The Complete History

First Published in 1995 by
INDEPENDENT MUSIC PRESS

Edited by Martin Roach
Overviews by Pat Gilbert
Proofing by Kaye Dunn
Cover by Sharon Thornhill
Buzzcocks logo courtesy of Malcolm Garrett
Time Out Clipping courtesy of Time Out Magazine and Andrew Nicholds

British Library Cataloguing-in-Publication Data
A catalogue for this book is available from The British Library

ISBN 1-89-7783-05-1

Printed and bound by The Guernsey Press Co. Ltd., Guernsey, C.I.

Independent Music Press
P.O. Box 3616, London E2 9LN

PHOTOGRAPHS CREDITS: Plate 1: Phil Mason; 2&3: Paul Clegg; 4: Paul Clegg (top),
Pete Monks (bottom); 5&6: Pete Monks; 7&8: Chris Gabrin; 10&11: Pete Monks; 12: Peter
& Alison Jones; 13: Peter Towndrow; 14: Tony McGartland; Artwork on plate 15 courtesy
of Malcolm Garrett

BUZZCOCKS

THE COMPLETE HISTORY

By Tony McGartland

Independent Music Press
London

Acknowledgements

I would like to thank the following fans and friends who took an interest and were always willing to help: Dave Bentley, Andy Bernstein, Andy Blade, Rob Cain, John Cassidy, Bob Dickinson, Peter and Alison Jones, John P. Lennon, Tim Lyons, Gary McNeish, Margaret McNeish, Joan McNulty, Andy MacPherson, Phil Mason, Chris Metzlar, Mick Middles, Pip Nichols, Steve Perrin, Eric Ramsden, Dave Riching, Lee Shelley, Graham Tinney, Aisla Wall, Tony Wall, Keith Wilde.

Without the help of the following people the discography would have been impossible: Jeffrey Hall, who assisted with an extensive Buzzcocks discography with contributions from Pete Shelley, Gerald Witherington, Greg Earle, Stephan Gelinas, Stephen Mulrine and Angela Lamb. Martin Hannett and Dave Rowbotham RIP.

I would like to thank the following people for their patience and assistance in providing me with vital information that I so persistently requested: Carey Adams (Abbey Road Studio librarian), Margaret Brown (BBC Radio), Tim Chacksfield (EMI Records), Sylvia Cowling (Granada TV), Kevin Cummins, Guy De Launey (BBC Written Archives Centre), Raf Edmonds, Alan Fitzjohn (BBC TV), Keith Hopwood (Pluto Studio's, Cheshire), Andy Linaham (National Sound Archive), Jon Savage, Neil Somerville (BBC Written Archives Centre), Gail Rook (Granada TV) and Paul Roberts (Drone Studio's.

Lastly, without the following people this book would have been impossible: Richard Boon, Pete Monks, Jon Ormrod, and Franny Taylor. And, of course, Howard Devoto, Pete Shelley, Steve Diggle, Garth Davies, Steve Garvey, John Maher. Lastly, not forgetting Buzzcocks newest members, Tony Barber and Phil Barker.

Finally, a special word of thanks to Martin Roach and Independent Music Press for their support in committing this project to print.

This book is dedicated to my wife Mary and our four children Michelle, Sarah, Paul and Tony.

Author's Note

For many Buzzcocks fans, the band's split in 1981 was the end, and for this reason the very thought of a reunion was belittled by many. Buzzcocks had made such a massive contribution to the pop world, and many people feared that the fond memories would be tainted by a substandard return. With this in mind, I have written their history in two distinct sections. The first is up to and including the original split, and is an in-depth chronology. The second section is from 1989 to the present day, a period I have chosen to cover in the form of a gigography, which not only lists all their shows but also documents all recording activity under the various line-up changes.

The contents of this book are the result of almost four years research, using tour itineraries, personal diaries of both band and crew members, radio and television contracts, session sheets and conversations in depth with everyone involved with the band. The overviews are designed to give some degree of context for what Buzzcocks achieved, with the main text detailing these events in greater depth. In an attempt to maintain the accuracy of this book and the events recorded within it, some approximate dates have been extracted from comments made in interviews, such as "a few days later". However, 99.9% of the dates are accurate and in every instance are totally factual.

Introduction

Buzzcocks' 1979 compilation *Singles Going Steady*, is without doubt one of the greatest punk albums of all time. Released two years before the band split, it was a distillation of everything uncommonly endearing about the Mancunian punk pop quartet: their wit, their romanticism and their ability to play fast, sardonic and timeless new wave tunes.

Sounds once said of them "There's no posing, no gobbing, no half-baked ideas of punkismo - just energy, presence and commitment. They sing because they have something to say." What the Buzzcocks said struck a chord with every teenager in the country. Indeed, the band - whose legendary debut EP 'Spiral Scratch' was the first truly DIY punk record - were one of those glorious young groups that brought alive all the drama of the teenage mag letters pages. Every track they ever recorded was a hormonally unstable youth anthem, simultaneously presenting the ups and downs of adolescent life.

While other bands sang about high society call-girls, Buzzcocks were still celebrating the pleasures of a swift masturbatory indulgence. Even in 1979, when the Clash were cruising in their (borrowed) 'Brand New Cadillac', Pete Shelley and the boys were still waiting for a night bus to take them home.

Yet though the characters who narrated Buzzcocks blistering punk pop ejaculations may have been forever sixteen (again), the maturing process of the outside world was always in danger of destabilising the band's career. Many of the greatest groups have thrived on internal tension, but Buzzcocks never looked more dangerous than when they were in a tight, harmonious unit.

In retrospect, this didn't happen until the recording of their first album, *Another Music In A Different Kitchen* in 1977. Around then, the band stabilised into the classic line-up we recognise today: Pete Shelley (vocs), Steve Diggle (guitar), Steve Garvey (bass) and John Maher (drums). Before that, two major figures had passed through their ranks - Howard Devoto (later of Magazine) and Garth Davies - but although their stints with the group were mercurial and exciting, they couldn't match the thrill and competence of the legendary 1978 set-up.

It was during this period that the band produced their best material, which capitalised on the early youth club bluster of classics like 'Orgasm Addict', 'Oh Shit!', and 'What Do I Get?' and catapulted the group into the public eye, perfectly capturing the ringing anthemic barrage of their live sets. Pete Shelley's camp, coquettish stage persona and dry Mancunian drawl gilded the Buzzcocks songs with the same magical veneer that Johnny Rotten's snarl added to the Pistols or Joey to the Ramones. Listening to Shelley's hiccuping about "butcher's assistants and bell-hops, winos and heads of state" was always like watching a beautiful pop art painting materialising before your eyes - sharp, life-affirming, funny - yet underneath there was hidden frustration.

By the time the group had released their second album, *Love Bites* and scored more hits with the all time classic 'Ever Fallen In Love?', 'Promises' and 'Everybody's Happy Now', the ironic truth was beginning to reveal itself. Confined by the band's simple rock set-up, each member was itching to experiment with outside projects, which within months they had embarked upon. Their third studio album, *A Different Kind Of Tension*, may have been a cry for help, yet the inventiveness of the music it contained overshadowed the growing unease among its creators. 'Paradise' and 'I Don't Know What To Do With My Life' were savagely invigorating songs, though sadly their effortless punk majesty wouldn't be matched again. An aborted fourth album and record company troubles brought Buzzcocks to an abrupt halt in early 1981, leaving Shelley to spiral into the darkness of depression.

But the band's split only heightened their reputation as one of the brashest and most melodic punk bands ever, and their clear and widespread influence made them look the most relevant punk band to what was happening in the 80's. So relevant, in fact, that they reformed in 1989, and have since become a massive live draw and a recording force to deal with, judging by their superb 1992 studio album *Trade Test Transmissions*. Pete Shelley once talked of "nostalgia for an age yet to come" - luckily with Buzzcocks still alive and frothing, that era still exists in the distant future.

1970-1975

Long before Buzzcocks formed in 1976, there were no romantic pseudonyms or ultra-sharp punk-pop songs like 'What Do I Get?' and 'Everybody's Happy Nowadays', neatly redefining the borders along which wit and fast guitars collided — all that was half a decade and an inspirational gig by the legendary Sex Pistols away. Instead, there was just a quartet of northern grammar school boys, with very ordinary names like Peter McNeish, Howard Trafford, Steve Diggle and Garth Davies, who shared an interest in late '60s American garage bands like the Velvet Underground and Stooges, and the wired, ground-breaking, home-grown sounds of Bolan, Bowie and, of course, The Beatles.

As with most of the other youngsters who made their name with the New Wave, their road to success was pitted with all kinds of embarrassing escapades, including the obligatory stints in dodgy sixth-form cover bands and earnest no-hoper rock outfits. In retrospect, Peter McNeish — soon to be known to the world as Pete Shelley — enjoyed a pre-punk history less cringe-worthy than that of many of his contemporaries, but there are certain moments which are probably best forgotten. It's hard to imagine that Shelley would want anyone to hear the home recordings of the 1973 teenage bluster of his rock group, Jets Of Air. The same would also be true of Howard Trafford's (later 'Devoto') piano playing with the fleeting Ernest Band.

But without these teenage experiences, it's unlikely that Shelley and Devoto would have been ready to realise their own punk vision after witnessing the bruising and chaotic onslaught of the Sex Pistols at two early 1976 gigs in London. Indeed, some of the Buzzcocks' debut album material had already been road-tested by Jets Of Air, who played slower, but nonetheless recognisable versions, of 'Love You More', 'Nostalgia' and 'Sixteen Again'. More curious still, Pete Shelley's classic electro '80s synth-pop solo track, 'Homosapien', dated from 1974.

Indeed, the mid-70s music scene shaped the new wave much more than was ever credited at the time. In the years since punk, a myth has prevailed that the period between 1970 and 1975 was artistically barren, yielding little else but the interminable wailing of ten-minute Led Zeppelin-style guitar solos and rambling rock operas. There's an element of truth in that, but a trip to the reissue section of any record shop reveals a very different story.

True, punk was born out of a frustration with manufactured teen-groups like the Bay City Rollers, as well as with Mercury and RAK's roster of ageing, consumer-friendly pop'n'roll outfits like Suzie Quatro, Mud, Showaddywaddy, The Rubettes and Smokie. Things weren't too hot at the 'serious' end of rock either, with The Who and Led Zeppelin losing their early majesty through years of chemical indulgence, and progressive rockers like Genesis, Mike Oldfield and the post-Syd Barrett Pink Floyd abandoning themselves to pseudo-symphonic masturbatory hell. Stateside, too, the music biz seemed to be stranded, as cocaine-fuelled record company moguls fawned over pompous, self-indulgent Album Orientated Rock acts such as Grateful Dead and the dreaded Jefferson Starship. In retrospect, these stultifying elements of the music scene were all symptoms of a much larger malaise — the much-talked about '70s hangover from the heady days of '60s counter-culture, when no one was worried about the price of too much free love and dodgy brown acid. This knowledge somehow made it all seem worse.

But the early '70s wasn't all bad — far from it, in fact. As teenagers, Pete Shelley, Howard Devoto and Steve Diggle existed at a time when pop music was more varied and inspiring than it would be again for several years to come. Weaving in and out of the studied tedium of the tight-trousered end of rock were those two great Bohemians of Brit-pop, Marc Bolan and David Bowie, both of whom had survived the late '60s to make a string of original, glamourous and wonderfully idiosyncratic rock albums, blurring their sexual identity and glittering themselves up along the way. With Bolan, Bowie and their friends Roxy Music, Sweet and even Slade, rock'n'roll suddenly became theatre, and everyone waited for the next costume change with baited breath.

Equally dramatic was the early '70s 'Kraut Rock' scene, which centred around a collection of German avant-garde artists who crafted the kind of quirky, synthesised soundscapes later to influence Bowie's *Heroes* and *Low* albums from 1976 and 1977 respectively. Groups like Can, Faust and Tangerine Dream — and to a lesser extent the solemn, monolithic industrialists, Kraftwerk — revolutionised the role of the synthesiser, and made challenging, often discordant music, that flew in the face of traditional rock structures. Kraftwerk took anti-rock notions a step further, using the synthesiser's austere sounds to articulate a sense of coolness and detachment, hinting at emotionally stark future worlds. Evidently, Pete Shelley was a fan, as in 1974 he recorded various doomy electronic sounds in the front room of his home, which later appeared on his 1981 solo record, *Sky Yen*. His first proper solo LP, 1981's *Homosapien* was highly technology-orientated, too.

More immediately relevant to punk, though, was the intense renewal of interest during the period in back-to-basics rock'n'roll, especially on the underground London music scene. As early as 1969, musicians who'd become famous in the '60s were expressing a desire to return to the simple R&B and rockabilly sounds that had inspired them to pick up guitars in the first place. Chief among these were The Beatles, who even planned to release an album called *Get Back*, which would be heavily indebted to the vintage 12-bar music of their heroes Chuck Berry, Little Richard and Elvis. In the event, it didn't happen (though the title-track escaped as a single), but it was indicative of a prevailing notion shared by bands as diverse as Kinks and Procol Harum that nothing beat a bit of old-style boogie.

With the advent of rock operas like Tommy, and bloated, self-indulgent progressive rock, more people decided to 'get back', and by 1974, bands like Dr. Feelgood, the Count Bishops and the 101ers had started playing a thrashy, super-charged version of old-fashioned rock'n'roll in pubs in and around London. This, of course, was the great Pub Rock, a much-maligned beast whose proponents included early incarnations of The Damned (then Johnny Moped), the Vibrators and, in spirit if not in style, The Stranglers. Lead singer of the 101ers was one John Mellor, better known as Joe Strummer, who played the dirtiest, tinniest, most amateur three-chord thrash most people had ever witnessed, and at deafening volume, too. He was the son of a British ambassador, who'd been an envoy to Turkey and Mexico, but you'd never have guessed it from Joe's strange, slurring voice and salt-of-the-earth manner. When the other future Clash founders, Mick Jones and bassist Paul Simonon, saw the 101ers live, they knew Joe was the man to front their own Mod-rock group.

Yet although pub rock, glam and the left-over spirit of '60s radicalism turbo-charged punk, and the dull, boring, indulgent stadium rock of Genesis and Boston afforded it a vacuum in which it could thrive, the New Wave was most directly inspired by something else — the New York punk scene of 1974-1975. A 1975

NME feature gave the first exciting snapshot of a city in which a bunch of gawky, bubblegum-chewing long-hairs were playing a brand of brash, beefy, garage rock, which had all the passion and attitude of The Yardbirds, The Stones and The Kinks in the mid-'60s. It was young, it was gormless, it was loud and it said "Fuck You!", and the key players were the New York Dolls, the Stilettos (with Debbie Harry of Blondie), Television, Talking Heads and The Ramones, with the eye of the hurricane usually being the CBGB's club. Overshadowing the whole scene, though, was the spectre of Iggy Pop's band, The Stooges, who together with the MC5 from Detroit had closed the '60s with a thunderous, misanthropic and menacing take on rock, the perfect antidote to wide-eyed hippie idealism and sophisticated pop. A veteran of several mental institutions, Iggy Pop was the coolest, skinniest and most slack-jawed 'punk' on the block, and his was the attitude — self-laceration was a favourite — that prompted the word 'punk' (meaning worthless trash) to be applied to the scene.

Godfathers of punk The Stooges and the MC5, and the fastest of their young charges, The Ramones, had a particularly profound impact on the British scene, with all three inspiring in varying degrees the Pistols, The Clash, The Damned and, yes, Buzzcocks (a very early incarnation of which covered Iggy's 'Your Pretty Face Has Gone To Hell'). Indeed, Buzzcocks couldn't have existed without what had gone before, self-consciously pinching their 60mph tempos from The Ramones, their sneers from the Pistols and their art-school swagger from the Velvet Underground. But those brilliant songs, which were already being written by Pete McNeish when he was working as a computer operator in the mid-'70s, well, they were all their very own.

Armed with experience, ideas and the desire to be the greatest, wittiest, most romantic punk-pop band in the world, young Peter McNeish and Howard Trafford stumbled through the early months of 1976 knowing that the British music scene was about to blow up in the nation's face.

1970

Jan 4th
A 15 year old Peter McNeish picks up a guitar his father had bought for his younger brother Gary's tenth birthday. Peter's New Year

resolution had been to keep a diary and the entry on this day reads "Today I will start to learn to play the guitar." His prime influence is *The Beatles Songbook*, assisted by playing along to the second-hand Beatles' records he had bought. His mother Margaret remembers "Every day after school he would be in his room with the guitar, teaching himself how to play." The diary is forgotten about after a few weeks.

Oct 3rd
McNeish attends his local youth club, where he listens to the *Led Zeppelin II* album with friends.

Dec 21st
Howard Trafford and Richard Boon are in a comedy group at Leeds Grammar School named The Ernest Band after their headmaster. Trafford plays piano and Boon the Jaw Harp, both sufficiently well to perform at the Christmas High School hop. Trafford was brought up in Nuneaton and Leeds.

1971

May 16th
Peter McNeish is in the audience at the Free Trade Hall, Manchester to see T. Rex, and is delighted to notice Marc Bolan wearing a guitar strap similar to his own.

May 17th
At the age of 16, McNeish starts writing his own material. His first ever song is called 'Yesterday Night'.

June 7th
A 16 year old Steve Diggle buys a Spanish guitar for £6 and starts practising in the Coronation Street style house where he lives in Moston. Having been born in Rusholme, before moving in his early years to Bradford, Diggle has now lived back in Manchester for two years. With his new instrument, he learns a few chords from a neighbour who plays Lindisfarne covers on the local pub circuit. Diggle is heavily influenced by John Lennon but gets a more immediate buzz listening to the thrashing guitar sound of The Who's Pete Townshend. Diggle's dad soon buys him an old Hayman bass guitar and a 120 watt Sound City amplifier - he

makes his own crude but effective speaker cabinet with wood that costs him £4.

June 13th
At Leigh Boys Grammar School, (Leigh is a mining and cotton town) a play for fifth and lower sixth form pupils features a rock band as part of the story-line. This brings together various school friends, all with an interest in music - Mick Reay, Keith Wilde and Tony Wall. Various drummers join and leave the band, disgruntled with the set list which includes covers of Free, Deep Purple and Jimi Hendrix. For the duration of the play they rehearse in the school hall.

On the last day of the play another guitarist, Peter McNeish joins the band. With the school hall no longer available, their lack of rehearsal space is solved by a friend in the year above, who likes the band and offers them space on his father's farm. During the summer, they rehearse in a cow shed at Naylor's Farm in Astley, near Leigh.

Despite the play being over, they are determined to stay together. They call themselves Kogg and play several gigs, including an NSPCC Benefit in a garden in Risley, an open-air concert in Bolton and at the village hall in Culcheth, before breaking up.

Nov 28th
At the age of 13, Steve Garvey buys his first record - 'Jeepster' by T-Rex, which this week rises to No. 2 in the charts. Although initially a Beatles fan, by the early seventies the Fab Four have been replaced as his heroes by Marc Bolan. With school friend Geoff Foster, a Marc Bolan look-alike, Garvey starts playing guitar and trying to get a band together. Garvey's best friends Martin Bramah and Tony Friel join the fledgling outfit but eventually leave to form a new band called The Outsiders, that later becomes The Fall.

1972

Feb 9th
McNeish buys a 'Starway' electric guitar which he had seen in the shop window of Magnall's Music store in his hometown, complete with a cardboard case for £18. Sometime later, he buys his first amplifier.

Sept 3rd
Howard Trafford goes to Bolton Institute of Technology to study Psychology and later, The Humanities.

Sept 11th
At the age of 17, Diggle starts work at Mountfords Iron Foundry in Bradford, training as a forge-man. He is only interested in music, but needs the money in order to buy a decent guitar. Part of his training at the foundry requires him to attend day-release, which fortunately means he can slip home at dinner time to play his guitar. Being a mod, and a fan of The Who, he is the proud owner of three scooters. After four or five months in the foundry he leaves and enrolls at Oldham Technical College where he studies English and Sociology O level.

1973

Jan 12th
In the aftermath of Bramah and Friel's departure, Garvey settles for a three piece band. He moves to bass and vocals, leaving Geoff Foster on guitar with Paul Adams on drums. Calling themselves Jawbone Hill, they play their first gig at a Working Men's club in their hometown of Prestwich, Manchester. They play three numbers, comprising the two Cream covers 'Sunshine Of Your Love' and 'White Room', and a third composition of their own.

Feb 26th
McNeish befriends a man at a youth hostel where they sit around and make their own entertainment, usually playing guitar. McNeish writes a song about the man's girlfriend, whom he had never met, called 'Maxine'.

Mar 3rd
Steve Christie is drumming with a band formed by guitarist Robert Francis Drake, and also featuring his friend Garth Davies. McNeish, who is in the year above them at Leigh Boys Grammar School, attends one of their rehearsals and asks Christie to come back to his house and rehearse with him instead.

Mar 17th
Diggle buys himself an 'Antoria' Les Paul copy guitar and starts

writing his own songs. He connects two cassette recorders together enabling him to overdub a second guitar track. One of the songs he writes and records is called 'I Might Need You'.

Apr 23rd
As a member of the Sixth Form Drama group, McNeish is in the cast of a school play called *The Bull Leapers* based on the ancient Greek legend of Minos, Theseus and Ariadne. The play runs for a week with McNeish acting the part of a guard.

McNeish writes 'I Just Can't Live' which he describes as a "tongue in cheek love song".

May 10th
McNeish forms Jets Of Air, taking the name from a phrase he heard in a Physics lecture. The band consist of McNeish on an Eko 12-string acoustic, Tony Wall (from Kogg) on guitar, Steve Christie on drums, and another friend, Garth Davies on bass.

May 26th
Jets Of Air play their debut gig at All Saints Church Hall in Leigh, paying for the hire of the hall with surprisingly good ticket sales. Their set consists of covers of David Bowie, Roxy Music, Velvet Underground and McNeish's own compositions, which in later years would become Buzzcocks classics.

June 12th
Jets Of Air play Bolton Secondary School. Keith Wilde, who played with McNeish in Kogg, is in the audience.

McNeish attends a lunch-time computer course at school. Most of the class drop out but Peter keeps going back.

Aug12th
McNeish gets a summer job as an exhaust fitter but gives up after two weeks.

Sept 16th
One Sunday afternoon, Davies brings his reel to reel recorder to Naylor's Farm and Jets Of Air tape themselves during rehearsal. Tracks recorded include cover versions of The Beatles' 'Back In The

USSR', Roxy Music's 'Editions Of You' and 'Remake, Remodel', Velvet Underground's 'White Light, White Heat' and several Bowie numbers - 'Hang On To Yourself/Jean Jeanie/John, I'm Only Dancing/Queen Bitch and Suffragette City'. Using his 12-string acoustic guitar fitted with a pickup, they also record two of McNeish's own compositions, entitled 'Telephone Operator' and 'I Just Can't Live'. McNeish suggests they record another track called 'Paradise', but they don't. Instead, this track finds its way onto their third album *A Different Kind Of Tension*.

During a break between numbers McNeish offers a few lines from 'Yesterday Night', the first song he ever wrote.

Oct 3rd
Peter McNeish fails his driving test.

Oct 20th
Jets Of Air play a gig in Culcheth which they promote themselves. Soon after, they play another show (which they record themselves) at a school in Walkden, the transport for which is a Sunshine Coach.

1974

Mar 2nd
McNeish records various electronic sounds in the front room of his home. These recordings are later used on *Sky Yen*, released through his own Groovy Records label in 1980.

Apr 10-12th
McNeish writes 'Pusher Man', 'Just One Of Those Affairs', 'Keat's Song', and 'Yesterday's Not Here'. These tracks are eventually released seven years later on his solo album *Homosapien*.

Aug 19th
Trafford buys as many Velvet Underground albums as he can find in a second-hand record stall.

Sept 4th
Malcolm Garrett attends Reading University where he is studying Typography, Psychology and The Humanities.

1975

Jan 4th
McNeish writes 'Love You More' about a girl he is going out with who works at Woolworth's in Bolton.

McNeish goes to the Bolton Institute of Technology to study a HND Course in Electronics. Howard Trafford requires electronic music for a video project he is working on and through the music society which Shelley has set up (to enable him to listen to more Kraftwerk), they meet up. Trafford and McNeish were previously only vague acquaintances, with Trafford not even being aware that McNeish played music.

May 23rd
Jets Of Air are finding it increasingly difficult to get concerts, and after repeated attempts to run a gig in Bolton prove unsuccessful, the band split up. At this stage their live set includes 'Love You More/Homosapien/I Don't Know What It Is/Just One of Those Affairs/Telephone Operator/Nostalgia/Sixteen Again'.

Sept 9th
Malcolm Garrett moves from Reading University to Manchester Polytechnic to start a three year course in Graphic Design. Here he meets Linder Sterling, who is one year above him and later moves in with Trafford.

Later in the year, Trafford places an advert on the Bolton Institute notice board which reads: "Wanted - people to form a group to do a version of Sister Ray" (the notice was also rumoured to contain a reference to euphonium players). As a big Velvet Underground fan, McNeish knew all their work, and so he phones Trafford. Whilst McNeish and Trafford work out cover versions of Stooges' songs like 'Your Pretty Face Has Gone To Hell', and 'The True Wheel', practising at parents' homes, various other musicians join and leave. The unnamed band never actually play but McNeish and Trafford keep in touch.

Oct 7th
Trafford introduces Richard Boon to McNeish at a party in Bolton. Boon remembers "He wore lots of bangles and too much mascara..."

1976

1976 — the year in which Britain enjoyed its hottest summer for a century, Labour leader Harold Wilson quit as prime minister, and Africa was ravaged by guerrilla conflicts — has passed into rock myth as the year that U.K. punk broke. In reality, the new wave's first tremor happened a couple of months earlier, on Thursday, 6th November 1975. That night, the Sex Pistols, whose line-up featured Johnny Rotten, Glen Matlock, Steve Jones and Paul Cook (guided by ex-New York Dolls manager Malcolm McLaren), played a support set at St. Martin's College of Art in central London, where Matlock was taking a part-time course. The band made such a racket that The plugs were pulled after only five songs, which included covers of The Who's 'Substitute' and the Small Faces' 'Whatcha Gonna Do About It?'. Soon after, they supported Eddie And The Hot Rods at The Marquee, and media reviewers watched in amazement as the Pistols ripped the headlines from the Hot Rods, with Rotten smashing chairs into the PA system whilst Pamela Rookie (later known as Jordan) stripped off to the waist. At the time of these astonishing early gigs, the best selling album in the country was by Jim Reeves, and a concerted media campaign had resulted in the re-entry into the charts of The Beatles.

It was an inauspicious start for a group that would revitalise rock music, but their decadent majesty was recognised by several people over these months: Stuart Goddard, — or Adam Ant, as he later styled himself — was the singer in Bazooka Joe, who saw the Pistols and was so impressed that he quit the very next day to form his own punk band, setting a precedent that would be followed by hundreds of musicians across the country. In the following months, Joe Strummer left the 101-ers, having been upstaged by the Pistols on the two occasions they opened for the five-star pub rock'n'rollers - he later said of Rotten's band "As soon as I saw them I knew rhythm and blues was dead"; Steve Bailey (later Severin) and Susan Janet Dallion started the amateur, discordant and completely wonderful Siouxsie And The Banshees after hearing about the Pistols' appearance in Bromley; Shane MacGowan quit his job as a barman in North London to kick-start the Nipple Erectors into action; William Broad set out on the road to becoming Billy Idol; and, last

19

but not least, Peter McNeish and Howard Trafford vowed to form Buzzcocks.

McNeish and Trafford had met at The Bolton Institute of Technology in 1975, and after reading an *NME* review of the Pistols' notorious support slot for Eddie And The Hot Rods, they arranged to see Rotten's band at a Friday night gig in High Wycombe, north-west of London. The pair duly borrowed a car for the weekend and travelled south, catching the group on the Friday night (which ended up in a huge punch-up, as would usually be the case) and at Welwyn Garden on Saturday (which didn't).

Both were gob-smacked by the band's sheer energy and Rotten's antagonistic stage presence, not to mention their savage version of the Stooges' 'No Fun'. During that weekend of intoxication by the punk spirit, a vision of their own group took shape in their imaginations, and by the time of their return to Manchester they had a suitably Sex Pistols-ish band moniker, and their own personal pseudonyms - Howard Trafford became 'Howard Devoto', and Peter NcNeish transformed into 'Pete Shelley'.

Over the next four months, Shelley and Devoto, along with scores of other nascent punks, threw themselves head-long into creating their own new wave groups. At this time, there were no rules: the idea was simply to recast yourself in the vein of the Pistols, and to play as loudly and as aggressively as possible. Within four months of their trip south, Shelley and Devoto had booked the Pistols for a gig in Manchester - another month later and Buzzcocks (completed by bassist Steve Diggle and 16-year-old drummer John Maher) had made their debut supporting them. In the audience that night were Ian Curtis, Peter Hook and Bernard Sumner, (who later formed Joy Division), Stephen Patrick Morrissey, Mick Hucknall and Tony Wilson. After this gig, the course of Manchester music was changed forever.

As the summer wore, and the temperature rose, punk bands began to excite a certain amount of media interest, garnering mixed reviews in the music press, which was often more interested in the sensational aspects of the new wave — the violence at gigs, the rowdy behaviour of the bands — than the music. Up until this time, punk was relatively unfocussed, but Pistols manager Malcolm McLaren attempted to present it as a concerted movement in September 1976, when he booked the 100 Club in London's Oxford Street for the infamous two-day punk festival, which showcased all the leading new wavers, including the Sex Pistols, The Clash,

Subway Sect and Siouxsie And The Banshees on the first night, and The Damned, Chris Spedding & the Vibrators, the Stinky Toys (from France) and Buzzcocks on the second. McLaren succeeded in creating a media event, with the *NME* taking up the punk cause, and the papers having a field day when their prejudices about punk violence were confirmed when Sid Vicious (then drummer with the Banshees) allegedly took a girl's eye out when a beer glass he hurled shattered on a pillar.

After this, punk rollercoasted, with groups getting banned from venues of all descriptions (including the 100 Club) and record companies seriously wondering whether the new wave could make them a quick killing. However, events were moving fast, and on October 22nd, the Damned issued their debut 45 (heavily influenced by the New York Dolls own debut) on the independent Stiff label, with the record selling 4,000 copies via mail-order before it was picked up for distribution by United Artists. In view of the major labels' hesitancy, independent releases looked as if they were the way forward. This appealed to Buzzcocks more than most - they had no intention of moving to London, and record companies seemed less than enthusiastic about making the jaunt north - this strong regional loyalty remained with Buzzcocks throughout their career, and reinforced their individuality within a movement that had more than its share of plagiarists (Shelley later said "We didn't hang out with any emerging scene, we just appeared there and started doing these things until it worked.") At this stage, a single could be recorded and pressed up for less than £1,000, which meant that, if suitable distribution could be found, the record might even make a profit. Buzzcocks didn't want to be left out, and having secured a loan from friends and family, they recorded four tracks just after Christmas 1976 for release on their own New Hormones label. The success of their debut 'Spiral Scratch' EP showed that a cheap self-released record was viable, and indeed preferable to major label avenues. This early success has led many observers to credit 'Spiral Scratch' with being the catalyst for the entire independent record label ethos.

1976 ended as it began, with the Pistols holding the trump punk card. On December 1st, they appeared on Thames TV's early evening current affairs programme, Today, hosted by veteran presenter Bill Grundy. The Pistols were obviously there to act up for the cameras, and Grundy played into their hands, chatting up hanger-on Siouxsie Sioux, and asking the band to "say something outrageous". Steve Jones did. With "dirty bastard" and a "fucking rotter" having been broadcast on prime time TV, the newspapers rolled off the press the next morning with tales of outraged viewers kicking their TV screens in - Rotten, Matlock, Jones and Cook instantly became household names.

January
Sat 24th
Diggle's musicianship has developed enough for him and a few friends try to form a band. They meet for rehearsals and play covers, including Black Sabbath's 'Paranoid', but they do not gel. Realising this, Diggle searches the 'Musicians Wanted' section in *Melody Maker* for a band in need of a guitarist.

February
Thurs 12th
Sex Pistols play support to Eddie And The Hot Rods at The Marquee Club in London. Neil Spencer of the *New Musical Express* is there to review the gig.

Thurs 19th
McNeish and Trafford read the review of the Sex Pistols gig in *NME*. They are impressed because the band play Iggy and the Stooges covers and the review quotes their lead singer Johnny Rotten saying "We're not into music, we're into chaos!"

Richard Boon, Trafford's erstwhile Grammar school collaborator in The Ernest Band, is now studying Art at Reading University. He invites both Trafford and McNeish down to London with the offer of accommodation for the weekend to see the Sex Pistols.

Fri 20th
Scanning the pages of *Time Out* magazine, a London 'what's on' guide, the three friends find no listing for the Sex Pistols. By chance, reading a review of a Thames television series called *Rock Follies* about a female rock group, they stumble upon the headline "It's the buzz, cock!" Trafford suggests that this phrase, with its hint of aural and sexual irregularity, would make a great name for a band.

That afternoon, a telephone call to the offices of the *NME* puts them in touch with the Sex Pistols' manager, Malcolm McLaren, who informs them of gigs that night and the following day. They plan to travel to both. In the evening, Sex Pistols play High Wycombe College of Further Education. McNeish, Trafford and Boon attend. Devoto remembers in *Product* how "Rotten was being very abusive and moody, I remember his shoes and a ratty red sweater. We thought they were fantastic."

Sat 21st
Sex Pistols play Welwyn Garden City. McNeish, Trafford and Boon again attend the gig. Hugely impressed by the band and Johnny Rotten, McNeish and Trafford both decide to change their identities. Peter McNeish becomes Pete Shelley (this would have been his mother's choice of name had he been born a girl), whilst Howard Trafford becomes Howard Devoto (the surname of a Cambridge bus driver recounted in a story by a philosophy tutor). They return to Manchester adamant to start a band themselves.

Sun 29th
Back in Manchester, Devoto and Shelley team up with former Jets Of Air bassist Garth Davies and rehearse for their planned debut gig at Bolton Institute of Technology on April 1st. Although as yet without a drummer, they still manage to put a set together containing a handful of original compositions, (one being 'Times Up') and several covers (Rolling Stones' 'Come On', The Stooges' 'True Wheel' and David Bowie's 'Diamond Dogs'). They also adopt Devoto's previously suggested moniker of Buzzcocks. Whilst sleeping over at Devoto's, an eager Shelley asks his friend about his commitment to the proposed band - Devoto replies "Yeah, I'm into living the life."

March
Mon 15th
Howard Devoto's birthday today, born 1952.

Mon 22nd
Pete Shelley is now working as a computer operator at Anderton House, Lowton near Leigh. The building is owned by the coal board. He leaves the job after a few months.

April
Thurs 1st
Buzzcocks make their debut at a social evening arranged for the textile students of the Bolton Institute, completing the line-up with an unknown drummer borrowed for the event from local band Black Cat Bone. They open their set with David Bowie's 'Diamond Dogs' followed by The Rolling Stones' 'Come On', which proves to be the last song of the night - the debut performance is so bad that the organisers pull the plugs after this second number. They are still paid their fee of £5.

Sat 17th
Pete Shelley's birthday today, born 1955.

Wed 21st
John Maher's birthday today, born 1960.

May
Tues 4th
Shelley and Devoto place an advert in the *New Manchester Review* for a drummer . Their plan is to have a band together to support the Sex Pistols at the Lesser Free Trade Hall, Manchester, (situated above The Free Trade Hall) which they book for June 4th at a cost of £32. As that day draws nearer, Davies and a drummer who had answered their advert both bottle out, the latter because he doesn't feel the rest of the band are good enough.

Fri 7th
Steve Diggle's birthday today, born 1955.

Sun 9th
Six weeks before joining Buzzcocks, a 16 year old John Maher is learning to play guitar, but after scanning the adverts in *Melody Maker* he realises that drummers are far more in demand, and promptly decides that this is what he will be.

Sat 22nd
Pete Shelley moves into a basement flat at 380, Lower Broughton Road, Salford. Although he has been living at his parents' home in Leigh, he was increasingly spending weekends at Devoto's flat at 364, Lower Broughton Road. Devoto had been renting

Poster for Buzzcocks first ever gig,
at Bolton Institute of Technology, 1/4/76

'It's The Buzz, Cock!'

'Rock Follies', Thames TV's series about the life and hard times of a female rock group, begins its six-part run on Tuesday. Andrew Nicholds *reports . . .*

Dee: 'It's the buzz, cock. When you sing the rock music you get this buzz—it starts in your chest, maybe it's to do with the amplifiers or the microphones, I don't know, it's something electric, something about energy.

a room there from a Philosophy Lecturer at his college for some time. He replaced Paul Clegg.

Sun 30th
Sex Pistols play Reading University Art Department. The gig is booked and paid for by Boon, who soon withdraws from the musical side completely and later in the year goes on to manage Buzzcocks.

June
Fri 4th
Sex Pistols play Lesser Free Trade Hall, Manchester. Since Davies and the drummer who had responded to their advert have both bottled out, the band are unable to make their planned debut. Their place is quickly filled by The Mandala Band from Blackburn, and the show plays to 100 people, each paying 50p each. Instead, Diggle has arranged to meet a guitarist outside the venue, totally unaware of what is happening inside. Sex Pistols manager, Malcolm McLaren is hustling kids inside, including Diggle. Pete Shelley is doorman for the evening and when Diggle announces himself as a bass player wanting to form a band, Shelley quickly introduces him to Devoto.

Sat 5th
Devoto calls Diggle and asks him to attend a rehearsal the following day.

Sun 6th
Howard Devoto (vocals), Pete Shelley (guitar) and newcomer Steve Diggle (bass) have their first rehearsal at 364, Lower Broughton Road.

Meanwhile, since realising the great demand for drummers, Maher has still been trying unsuccessfully to join several bands as a guitarist, but with his suspicions now confirmed, he hires a kit for £20 and soon after trades all his guitar equipment in to buy his own drum kit. He teaches himself by playing along to records in the front room of his house, but the neighbours are not impressed, so after several complaints he starts looking through the adverts in *Melody Maker*. He replies to one advert which reads "Girl, looking for musicians to get together and form a band" and, ironically, finds that she too is a drummer. Devoto replies to the same advert and is told by the girl that Maher may be more appropriate. He gets Maher's phone number, calls him up and arranges a meeting. Shortly after, just before Maher leaves his house to sit his Chemistry O level, Devoto calls round to ask if he would be interested in joining Buzzcocks, without an audition. On every Saturday between now and the debut gig, Maher rehearses with Devoto, Shelley and Diggle in the basement of Devoto's flat at 364, Lower Broughton Road, in preparation for the re-arranged debut gig, now on 20th July. It is a large terraced house, big enough for rehearsals, but the noise does little to please the neighbours.

A beleaguered neighbour of Devoto's offers the young band rehearsal space at St. Boniface's Church Hall, Frederick Road in Salford, of which he is the caretaker. It is a thinly veiled manoeuvre to eradicate the noisey band from his home life. They accept nonetheless.

Wed 16th
Maher decides against a job with the Methodist Insurance Company in Manchester and formally joins Buzzcocks.

Tue s 22nd
Boon leaves Reading University after four years studying Art. Putting off vague plans to study a post-graduate teacher training course, he moves in with Devoto in Lower Broughton Road: "I didn't really know what to do once I had graduated, there was a room available in this notorious house so I moved into it."

July
Mon 19th
Pete Shelley and Richard Boon enjoy a drink in Cox's Bar, the night before Buzzcocks' debut at Lesser Free Trade Hall.

Tues 20th
Buzzcocks (finally) play their first full gig at the Lesser Free Trade Hall supporting the Sex Pistols. Local glam rock thugs Slaughter and the Dogs also play. Songs from the set include 'Breakdown/Oh Shit!/I Love You, You Big Dummy/Times Up/I Can't Control Myself'.

Shelley buys a cheap Woolworths 'Audition' guitar especially for the pre-planned destruction of the gig to follow. At the end of the set,

LESSER FREE TRADE HALL

FREE TRADE HALL - PETER ST MANCHESTER

£1·00   TUESDAY 20th JULY   7·30pm   £1·00

SEX PISTOLS

WITH SLAUGHTER AND THE DOGS

BUT BUZZCOCKS

£1·00

TICKETS AT FREE TRADE HALL £1·00 BOOKING OFFICE

Poster for Buzzcocks second gig, supporting Sex Pistols at Lesser Free Trade Hall, 20/7/76

both Devoto and Shelley pull violently at the strings, ripping them from the new instrument, whilst Maher runs through the crowd and out into the night. A New Zealander friend of Devoto's called Mark Roberts makes an 8mm soundless film of the performance. Among those in the audience is Boon's friend from Leeds University, Sue Cooper, who becomes a close friend of the band and eventually moves up to Manchester to assist Boon at the New Hormones office.

After the gig, Buzzcocks meet Linder Sterling, a graphic artist who produces some early artwork for the band, using only her first name. Devoto and Linder soon start going out together. Through Linder, the band meet Malcolm Garrett, her friend from Manchester Polytechnic. This marks the beginning of a long association as Garrett produces the Buzzcocks logo and works on the band's visual presentation throughout their career. Meanwhile, despite selling 400 tickets at £1, Buzzcocks make a profit of only £10.

Sat 31st
Because McLaren had ferried many journalists to the Lesser Free Trade gig from London, Buzzcocks were seen on their full debut by many top writers. Consequently, a review of Buzzcocks' debut gig appears in *Sounds* under the headline "Anarchy In The UK". After seeing his name in print, Pete Shelley buys three copies.

August
Fri 6th
During rehearsals at St. Boniface's Church Hall, Shelley's guitar strap comes off and his guitar falls to the floor. He picks it up and throws it across the room, breaking it into two pieces.

After meeting a photographer called Phil Mason from the New Manchester Review, Devoto invites him to shoot some pictures of the Buzzcocks during one of the Church Hall rehearsals.

Thurs 12th
Buzzcocks play The Ranch Club, Manchester. The venue was originally a gay club, adjoining Foo Foo Lamaar's Palace, a drag artist's residence. The stage is in a small room inside Foo Foo Lamaar's club, from where the drag artist can be seen performing through a little hatch, a closed door legacy from the club's gay origins. *Shy Talk*, the original Manchester fanzine, was sold from the

hot pie counter, and the club itself became a strong punk venue. Tonight, after just a few numbers, one of the club's heavies slowly circles around the band. After a few circuits around the bemused band, they stop and the heavy says to Howard "Are you the boss? Well, Foo Foo says you've got to stop, it's too loud!"

Fri 13th
Buzzcocks travel in a van to London's Notre Dame Hall at the invitation of Sex Pistols' manager Malcolm McLaren. He offers them a photo session with *Bravo* magazine who are in London to cover "punk rock". Although the Sex Pistols mime for their session, Buzzcocks actually set up their equipment and play several numbers live. One of the photographs later appears in an *NME* feature (Feb. 5th 1977).

Sat 28th
Buzzcocks play The Commercial Hotel, Stalybridge, a gig organised by themselves through Devoto's acquaintance with the owner, Mrs. Mately, whom he met whilst compiling the 'pub rock' listings for the *New Manchester Review*. This connection does not earn them an easy gig however - Devoto is booed off the stage for wearing green fluorescent socks and red slippers by the local crowd.

Sun 29th
Buzzcocks play support to the Sex Pistols at the 'Screen On The Green', Islington, north London, partly as a return gesture by McLaren. Paul Clegg drives the van south. The Clash also play their debut gig tonight on the same bill (they had actually debuted on August 13th, but this was a closed performance at their manager's rehearsal studio in Chalk Farm for the press only - this Islington gig was their first public appearance), but the London bands fail to enter into the spirit of punk solidarity and exclude the Northerners from most of the proceedings. Buzzcocks play 'Breakdown/Friends of Mine/Times Up/Orgasm Addict/Peking Hooligan/Lester Sands/Oh Shit!/You Tear Me Up/Love Battery/I Can't Control Myself'. The set contains Shelley/Devoto compositions which remain firm live favourites throughout Buzzcocks' career.

An audience recording of this Buzzcocks performance includes a very early Devoto composition called 'Peking Hooligan'. Devoto wrote the song after reading an article in *The Guardian* about the rise of juvenile delinquency in China. On the same tape, a strong Mancunian voice can be heard saying "Has yours got sugar in it?"

Sounds columnist Giovanni Dadamo reviews the Buzzcocks performance as "rougher than a bear's ass!"

September
Tues 14th
A 15 year old Andy Blade earmarks Manchester as the city where he is going to debut his band Eater. He decides against a gig with Slaughter And The Dogs and on the advice of producer Martin Hannett goes looking for Buzzcocks. He calls Devoto and they arrange to meet in a Wimpy Bar in Manchester. When asked how he will be recognised, Devoto replies, "I'll be wearing a pink carnation." They meet and make plans for the gig at Holdsworth Hall, the following week.

Mon 20th
Buzzcocks play Holdsworth Hall, Deansgate, Manchester. As planned, Eater make their debut, and despite Buzzcocks' prior experience, the two bands toss a coin to see who will headline - Eater win (Shelley later said "Should have made it the best of three..."). Devoto has his hair bleached for the gig and wears nail varnish, as well as Vivienne Westwood leather trousers. With Buzzcocks finished, the Manchester crowd heckle the London headliners so much that after only their third number the bass player walks off, leaving the band to continue without him. Tonight is Boon's first official night as Buzzcocks' manager, most of which he spends taking money on the door. Also, Franny Taylor, a flatmate of Shelley's, sees the band for the first time, and during the following year joins the Buzzcocks road crew.

This Buzzcocks gig coincides with the first night of 'The 100 Club Punk Festival' in London, featuring the Sex Pistols, The Clash as well as Subway Sect and Siouxsie And The Banshees, who both make their debut.

Tues 21st
The second day of 'The 100 Club Punk Festival' sees Buzzcocks play last on the billing, but unfortunately by then most of the audience have gone home. The festival ends with Buzzcocks

disappearing into the audience and Pete Shelley's guitar still on stage feeding back.

Sat 25th
A few weeks before their first recordings are due to be made at Revolution Studios in Stockport, Devoto uses a reel to reel machine to record a rehearsal in the basement at 364, Lower Broughton Road.

Tues 28th
Buzzcocks get their first mention in the seminal fanzine *Sniffin' Glue*.

October
Sat 2nd
Melody Maker columnist Caroline Coon reports on the 100 Club shows, Britain's first punk rock festival. The three page article titled "Parade Of The Punks", mentions lead singer Devoto's orange hair, justifying his special hair style.

Fri 8th
Back in Salford, Buzzcocks play an unpublicised gig at St. Boniface's Church Youth Club, by way of repaying the Church Hall for allowing them so much rehearsal time. Since the majority of the gig's audience is so young, (only 8 or 9 years old) Devoto suggests they change the words of 'Oh Shit!' to 'Oh Spit!'. The six number set also features 'Fast Cars' being played for the first time. Diggle uses his bass amplifier to stop the bass drum sliding around. Meanwhile, several kids run around in circles, shrieking loudly as the band play.

Mon 18th
Buzzcocks record most of their set at Revolution, a small loft studio on Bramhall Lane in Stockport, for a total cost of £45. The resident engineer Andy MacPherson offers Shelley a brand new guitar from the studio, but he insists on using his broken 'Starway'. As Buzzcocks record everything live, the whole session only takes four hours, recorded through an AMEK 12:2:4 X Series mixing desk onto a Sony 2-track which was borrowed for the day. Later, MacPherson engineers the recordings in the attic of his flat.

Eleven out of twelve of these Revolution recordings are later unofficially released on the *Times Up* bootleg album which first appears in 1978.

Tues 26th
Buzzcocks rehearsals move from St. Boniface's Church Hall, Salford to Lifeline, a drug rehabilitation centre on Lower Mosely Street, Manchester. The centre is not safe enough for the band to leave any gear there, so they set up, rehearse, re-load the van and return home. Boon booked this rehearsal as one of his first jobs as manager.

November
Mon 8th
Buzzcocks play the Band On The Wall, Manchester, a jazz club in a public house which the *New Manchester Review* occasionally used for gigs like this, their second anniversary celebrations. Devoto introduces the band as "Buzzcocks, the best in good food!" Also on the bill are Bob Williamson, The Phantom Band and C. P. Lee of Albertos Y Los Trios Paranoia's.

During the set, Boon is at the bar when an old flat-mate from Reading University, Pete Monks, walks in. Monks asks him what he is doing there, Boon tells him he is managing the band on stage and the two watch the set. Pete Monks later becomes Buzzcocks' driver and tour manager.

A segment of Buzzcocks' gig at Band on the Wall, is featured in the opening intro of the bootleg album *Best In Good Food*. The compere's intro is taken from a flexi-disc given away with *Readers Digest*, featuring the 'Big Band' sound of Glenn Miller, but on this bootleg it is cleverly edited with Shelley's two-note lead solo from 'Boredom'.

Wed 10th
Buzzcocks play the Electric Circus in Rochdale Road, Collyhurst, Manchester, a heavy metal venue with Chelsea supporting. Shelley meets Ian Curtis (later of Joy Division) for the first time. This venue went on to establish itself as the premier punk club outside of London. The Circus was only closed down when local fire authorities slapped a restrictive 'fire safety limit' on it, making it financially unfeasible.

Sat 27th
NME carries a review of the Buzzcocks Band on the Wall gig, saying: "They're producing the most significant musical output of any new British rock band. Where they're going to go next is anyone's guess!"

Sun 28th
Buzzcocks play Electric Circus again, this time with Slaughter And The Dogs supporting.

December
Sat 4th
Pete Shelley records a selection of experimental sounds at home on a Bontempi organ. Four years later, in 1980, the New Hormones label plan to release these recordings on an album called *Cinema Music And Wallpaper Sounds* but the idea is abandoned. Two of these songs, 'It's Hard Enough Knowing' and 'I Don't Know What It Is' finally appear on Shelley's 1981 solo album *Homosapien*.

Thurs 9th
Buzzcocks play Electric Circus supporting the Sex Pistols on their infamous 'Anarchy Tour', replacing The Damned who have been kicked off the tour. This dismissal arose after Derby Borough Council had insisted the Pistols perform at a private afternoon meeting in front of the assembled dignitaries to decide if the band were suitable for the young people of their city to be exposed to. The Pistols don't turn up, but as The Damned agree to the council's terms, Malcolm McLaren decides they no longer have a place on the tour. This gives Buzzcocks a superb opportunity to feature on a classic tour. At this stage, they are clearly a band in the ascendancy, and yet tonight will prove to be the last gig vocalist Howard Devoto ever plays with the band.

Sat 18th
During rehearsals at Lifeline, each member of the band writes down their own choice of four tracks for the planned debut vinyl, the 'Spiral Scratch' EP. As yet, the band remain unsigned.

Sun 26th
Shelley writes 'What Do I Get?'

Tues 28th
Buzzcocks record the chosen four tracks at Indigo Studios, Gartside Street, Manchester with (soon to be) highly renowned producer Martin Hannett (known locally as Martin Zero, who would go on to be responsible for much of Joy Division's work). They met Hannett through the agency he ran in the same building as the

New Hormones office. The tracks are 'Breakdown/Times Up/ Boredom/Friends of Mine'.

Wed 29th
Shelley produces his own one-page fanzine called *Plaything*, written and typed in his bedroom. Fortunately, Shelley's brother Gary has borrowed a Xerox machine and this proves invaluable for reproducing the fanzine. So invaluable in fact, that when Gary returns the copier, the fanzine folds after only two issues.

PLAYTHING NO 2
3P

Whenever someone talks about the NEW WAVE they mean the 'new
wave' of music & musicians that have emerged & influenced the
scene in the last two years. The only new wave is in music.
It has succeeded & failed. Succeeded with a reapraisal of the
ideas, aims, & philosophies of a new set of musicians and of
audiences. It failed by our lack to separate the wheat from
the chaf and thinking that one battle wins the war.
The succees is due to action - the failiure due to apathy.
One wave does not make much headway up the beach.
If the tide is to turn then one wave must be followed by
another and so on until the cliffs start to crumble.
This is just the new wave of the turning tide. The next wave
will start from where this one has finnished. So don't slacken
off now, but slip into a higher gear. There still is a lot more
we can do.
    The NEW WAVE is not just about music. It is a challenge to
Consider every thing you do, think, and feel. For some it has
meant a change in fashion and in life style. But most of the
fashion has become cliched and most of the groups have even now
become boring old farts future tax exiles and full of crap such
as saying " I don't want to hear about politics, I just want to
have a good time. It's only rock & roll." But it's not only
rock & roll! If it was then what is all the fuss about it?
Politics is people & people is YOU
I'm not on about party politics not the NF or The Tories. I'm
talking about PERSONAL politics. The way that you react to the
people around you. The ways that you love them, fuck them, hate
them, slate them. Things like love, jealousy, hate, anger, sex ...
How often do you do some thing to some one & not know why you
did it?
    The NEW WAVE is like a spring clean. You were prepared to throw
out the rubbish in your wardrobe and your record collection.
So why not chuck out all the prides & prejudices cluttering
up your personality????
    Just think about how you react with other people.
    I'll write more when I think of what to say.

This is all I could think
of. Keep the new wave
NEW. Pete Shelley

1977

After the Bill Grundy incident, punk went well and truly public. Kids in provincial towns who'd never seen the Pistols, Buzzcocks and Clash could now read about them, and even buy a bona fide punk record in the guise of The Damned's blistering 'New Rose' 45. Yet with punk's new found celebrity also came a respectability of sorts. In October 1976, the Sex Pistols had signed to EMI, the company that had brought us The Beatles, while in January, The Clash, who'd always taken a radical political stance, stencilling their clothes with pseudo-terrorist slogans like "Sten Guns In Knightsbridge" and singing about dole queues, closed a deal with CBS worth a reported £100,000. By April, The Stranglers, who were already signed to United Artists, were selling copies of their debut album, *Rattus Norvegicus*, by the truck load, while The Jam had been snapped up by Polydor for a meagre £6,000 advance (which was quickly upped). Generation X soon signed a massive worldwide deal with Chrysalis, and in the charts all of the above were placed higher than the so-called traditional bastions of music such as 10cc, Rod Stewart and even The Beatles.

Early spring witnessed The Clash debuting with the trashy 'White Riot' and the Sex Pistols moving to A&M, having been chucked off EMI for their headline-hitting behaviour. After just a few weeks, the Pistols also got the boot from A&M, taking a healthy wedge with them.

Although confused by punk's many contradictory philosophies — was it all a scam, or did it have a serious message? — hundreds of music fans were smitten with its insolence, energy and spiky, trashy look. With Radio 1 DJ John Peel championing the punk cause, the sounds of the new wave were beamed all over the nation, and literally hundreds of bands like the Undertones, Stiff Little Fingers, the Ruts, the Rezillos and the Cure began cropping up in the provinces, adding to the wealth of bands formed by fringe-members of the original '76 punk scene, such as Generation X, 999, Chelsea, the Models, the Subterraneans, Eater, the Only Ones and Sham 69.

At the margins of all this activity, Buzzcocks looked on with a smirk, aware that they were in danger of getting left behind because of line-up problems and the lack of a decent deal. Already bands they had partly inspired were now headlining above them, such as The Clash. Their debut 'Spiral Scratch' EP had been instantly hailed a punk classic but its success perversely prompted the departure of Howard Devoto, who believed that, with this rattling agit-pop delight, he'd achieved everything he'd set out to do with the band. Buzzcocks were momentarily wrong-footed, but quickly steered themselves back on course. Recruiting Garth Davies — who'd previously played with Shelley in Jets Of Air — they set out with The Clash on the legendary 'White Riot' tour, before finalising a long-term deal with United Artists in the late summer. This deal came after a period of stasis, when A&R men were initially unsure of Buzzcocks, confused by their lack of conformity to the prototype they knew - a good example of this is the highly distinctive Buzzcocks artwork, designed by Malcolm Garrett (and Linder), which adorned every release and poster. However, after recording several demos for their first album, there were more upsets. Davies was becoming increasingly unreliable, and in October the Buzzcocks were forced to replace him with Prestwich-based bassist Steve Garvey. It had been a rough year, but finally, in October 1977, the band's first major label release appeared, the brilliant Shelley/Devoto composition, 'Orgasm Addict', which sold heavily, despite an airplay ban.

Meanwhile, the Sex Pistols were on something of a roll, having sabotaged the Queen's jubilee in the summer by kidnapping the No. 1 spot with their raucous anthem, 'God Save The Queen', and performing on a barge sailing past the Houses Of Parliament during the Jubilee celebrations on June 7th. As with Buzzcocks, their bassist, Glen Matlock, had to go because of internal friction, though his replacement Sid Vicious seemed to epitomise punk's anti-social image even better than his friend and band-mate, Johnny Rotten. Unfortunately, despite looking great, Sid couldn't play the bass very well, and Matlock was re-employed behind the scenes to finish off the bass parts to their notorious debut LP, *Never Mind The Bollocks*.

1977 was the year when punk went legit, when its idealism and antagonism were harnessed by experienced record company producers to make some of the most mercurial and invigorating music ever. It was also the time when commentators wondered whether it was in punk's interest to last. It was, by its very nature, an incendiary and revolutionary music, and like all successful rebellions, the seditionaries become the new establishment. 1978 would be a year in which punk would have to finally face up to its own contradictions.

January
Tues 4th
Without record company backing, Richard Boon and Howard Devoto desperately try to get the cash needed to press the debut 'Spiral Scratch' EP. Shelley's Dad starts them off with £250 from his Friendly Society account, after which they turn to Richard's University friend Sue Cooper. After explaining their dilemma over the phone, she agrees to loan them £100, (her parents' contribution to her University fees). The target figure for the EP is finally met by a contribution from Dave Sowden, another friend of Richard's, who was earning a regular wage teaching in London.

Fri 7th
Boon snaps the four Buzzcocks on a Polaroid camera for the cover of their 'Spiral Scratch' EP. The picture is taken at the Robert Peel statue in Manchester's Picadilly Gardens, with the four youths cramming to get into the picture.

With the necessary funds now available, Buzzcocks become the first punk band to form their own record label, New Hormones, on which they intend to release their debut vinyl (the label is apparently named after an earlier Devoto magazine: "I wanted them"). The record is pressed by Phonogram in a special one-off deal, but is "bagged and quality controlled" by the band themselves at Lower Broughton Road - as Shelley later said "we checked each and every one for scratches and stuff." Each record is accompanied by a leaflet saying "This is almost certainly going to be a limited edition release, there won't be much advertising." The release date is set for 29th January. On the day of arrival the band buy two bottles of cheap Spanish wine and toast their debut release, about which Shelley later said "It was meant to be very spontaneous, like a snapshot of what happened at that time. It was just something to show your grandkids."

New Hormones use the address of the *New Manchester Review* to receive mail at 182, Oxford Road. The band and their manager Richard Boon are regular visitors to these offices. Eventually, New

Hormones moves to 50, Newton Street in the city centre. Boon was ably assisted by Sue Cooper, Margaret Trotter and Peter Wright.

Sat 15th
Sounds news pages succinctly report the debut vinyl: "Buzzcocks are releasing a single on their own New Hormones label at the end of January and it will sell for £1."

Sun 16th
In an attempt to beat the record for the longest running D.J. broadcast, Picadilly Radio stages an event at Flanagan's in Oxford Street. During a set played by The Drones, Shelley jams with the band on a version of Steppenwolf's 'Born To Be Wild'.

Tues 25th
A planned Buzzcocks show at The Roxy Club, London is cancelled.

Sat 29th
The debut vinyl 'Spiral Scratch' is officially released, distributed through Rough Trade in London. Within four days it sells 1,000 copies, and rapidly becomes the best selling single in Manchester's Virgin Records store. Geoff Travis of Rough Trade said "It was the first independent record that people really wanted. We must have ordered hundreds of them." Hereafter, it is pressed in a series of small runs from January right through to the end of July 1977, eventually totalling 16,000. The band had needed to sell 600 copies to repay the loan.

The single is a repetitive, vibrant collection, led by Devoto's fake Cockney voice and drilled by their screeching guitars and two note guitar solos. In the Buzzcocks box set *Product*, released in 1989, Shelley said "Punk evolved from sub Heavy Metal played badly, fast riffs and singing over the top.We were just trying to get things to happen in a way that wasn't happening before."

NME publish a letter from Stephen Morrissey from Stretford, which reads "Buzzcocks differ in only one way from their contemporaries: they possess a spark of originality!" Apart from such public support, the band also receive backing in the media, with *Melody Maker* leading the way by saying "this is fast, sparse, intense and red hot with the living spirit and emotion of rock and roll."

Mon 31st
Martin Rushent joins United Artists as an assistant to Andrew Lauder in the A&R Department.

February
Wed 2nd
Despite the growing interest in the band, Howard Devoto leaves Buzzcocks. Pete Shelley commenting on Devoto's departure "When we started the group he just wanted to know what it was like being a rock star. Once he found out, he just left." Devoto had played a total of 11 gigs with Buzzcocks.

Devoto himself gave several reasons for leaving: "One was about finishing my college course, or at least giving it a reasonable shot after so many bloody years doing this whole educational lark. Another reason was the feeling that the band was going nowhere - we were in Manchester, people from record companies or for that matter anyone else just didn't come up to Manchester. We simply did not have people knocking on the door or turning up at gigs. In addition, the key thing that really changed everything was 'Spiral Scratch' coming out. We had 1000 pressed and were worried if we were going to sell enough copies to pay back everyone we had borrowed money from. The unexpected success of that record really pushed things up from first to top gear. Finally, there was also a part of me that wasn't too enthusiastic about there being so much punk rock music, suddenly it was everywhere. If I felt it had been going somewhere, I probably would have thought somewhat differently about the whole thing."

In the press at the time of leaving, Devoto was a little more obscure, saying "I'm tired of noise and short of breath" and that "what was once unhealthily fresh is now a clean old hat."

Buzzcocks consider replacing Devoto with local lad known only as Robert, who later became vocalist with The Prefects. After much discussion, they decide against it, feeling a new front man would be too drastic a change. This same week, The Clash's manager Bernard Rhodes phones Shelley up and asks him if he would be interested in leaving Buzzcocks to work with ex-Clash guitarist Keith Levine. Shelley turns the offer down.

Thurs 3rd
'Spiral Scratch' EP is played for the first time on BBC Radio 1's highly influential *John Peel Show*.

Sat 5th
NME features Buzzcocks' first major piece of publicity with a headline that reads "Teen Rebel Scores £250 From Dad." The Paul Morley article features a youthful Pete Shelley and a long haired Steve Diggle. It is still less than twelve months since, in the same music paper, Pete Shelley and Howard Devoto read the Sex Pistols review that inspired them to form the band.

Fri 11th
Buzzcocks place a notice in Manchester's Virgin record store which reads "Leading North-West beat combo require bass player who is pretty or competent, or pretty competent!" Steve Diggle moves to rhythm guitar and Garth Davies, Shelley's old school friend, re-joins the band as their new bass player. He uses a Hayman bass borrowed from Diggle, whose father had bought it for him in 1971. Shelley takes up lead vocals and guitar and the quickly re-shaped Buzzcocks rehearse heavily for their first gig without Devoto, a show at London's Harlesden Coliseum in early March.

Sat 12th
NME review Buzzcocks' 'Spiral Scratch' EP as "heavily New York influenced in style". *Melody Maker* columnist Caroline Coon comments "It has twisted its abrasive little way right through my soft, unsuspecting gut!"

Tues 15th
Pip Nicols rings Shelley to enquire about the bassist vacancy in Buzzcocks, and he informs her that Davies has already taken the job. However, Shelley is suitably impressed and passes her phone number on to Steve Perrin of 'The Distractions', who subsequently enlist Pip on bass.

Mon 28th
Buzzcocks are scheduled to play at London's 'Global Village' two-day punk festival with the Sex Pistols, The Clash, The Damned and Slaughter And The Dogs. The festival is cancelled.

March
Fri 11th
Buzzcocks play Harlesden Coliseum, London, supporting The Clash, their second gig in the capital. This is the band's first gig without Devoto, but they are not alone - The Slits also make their debut. They are driven to London by Pete Monks, his first night as 'official' driver for the band. Another friend, Eric Ramsden is also there as roadie. The intense rehearsals and Buzzcocks' individuality set the new band apart from their contemporaries - there is no posturing, no gobbing, no pretension, with Shelley's laconic Mancunian accent distinctively introducing their snatches of vibrant energy and commitment.

The set list consists of 'Fast Cars/What Do I Get?/Sixteen Again/No Reply', (all new numbers), and 'Times Up/Boredom/Friends Of Mine/Orgasm Addict/You Tear Me Up/Get On Our Own/Love Battery'.

Howard Devoto attends the gig. He is down on the guest list as 'Mole Rothman'.

The band wear their 'Mondrian' style shirts for the first time made by Janey Collings, yet another friend of Boon's from Reading University. Later, she is responsible for the silk-screen printed, two - tone green 'What Do I Get?' shirts. These early shirts set the trend of the majority of Buzzcocks' visual tone, and set them clearly apart from The Clash, who by now were adopting their military zippered gear, and indeed this one aspect of Buzzcocks clearly separated them from their contemporaries - their music was not the only focus of the group. All packaging and visual aspects of the band were designed by Malcolm Garrett, with input also from Linder and Boon as well. Thematically, the artistic side to Buzzcocks referred at every juncture to Fine Art, such as the work of Kasimir Malevich, Andy Warhol, Peter Phillips, John Heartfield, Jan Tschichold and Piet Mondrian to name a few. Aspects of Beatles-ish design also cropped up occasionally, such as the covert resemblance to their *White Album* on the embossing of *Love Bites*. Posters and visuals regularly featured kettles, toasters, and other household appliances, reflecting the close attention to detail which Garrett, Linder and Boon pursued through reference to actual lyrics.

This highly distinctive visual focus was complemented by the band's choice of titles for records and tours. Titles such as 'Entertaining Friends' fuelled the band's attempts to demystify the whole record producing process, typified most directly by the name of the 1989 box set *Product*. Like their attendance at the birth of the independent record label, Buzzcocks are seen by many to have ushered in an era of band visuals unknown at the time.

Sat 12th
Buzzcocks play at The Vault, Brighton. The gig is set up by friends of the band, Sue Cooper and Richard Swales, who later became The Poison Girls, but who appear as support to Buzzcocks tonight under no name.

Fri 18th
Buzzcocks play Liverpool, Eric's.

April
Fri 1st
A Buzzcocks interview features in Issue 1 of the Manchester fanzine *Ghast Up*, conducted in The Abercrombie public house near Deansgate, by Mick Middles and Martin Ryan. Shelley wandered into the pub wearing an orange kagool and a pair of brushed denim flares.

Sat 2nd
Buzzcocks play The Roxy Club, London. This is the band's debut gig at The Roxy, with Johnny Moped, X-Ray Spex, Wire, and Smax also on the bill. A Transit van with around sixteen Manchester punks leaves from The Ranch Club to drive to London for the live recording of *The Roxy Club* album. On board are Francis Taylor, Paul Morley, Joan Juice, Denise, Suzanne, Allan, Ian and other original Buzzcock fans. The band play 'Orgasm Addict/No Reply/Get On Our Own/Breakdown/Fast Cars/What Do I Get?/Friends Of Mine/Sixteen Again/Love Battery/Times Up/Boredom', and then encore with 'Love Battery'.

After the gig, Shelley decides to travel back to Manchester in the van, but ends up spending most of the night sleeping and messing about at Scratchwood Service Station.

Sun 3rd
Mike Thorne mixes the Buzzcocks performance from the previous night's gig, which was recorded by Manor Mobile.

Mon 4th
Buzzcocks concert at Band On The Wall is moved to May 2nd.

Tues 5th
Boon repays Sue Cooper back the £100 loan which was used to assist the financing of the 'Spiral Scratch' EP.

Thurs 7th
Buzzcocks make their television debut on Tony Wilson's *What's On* programme, transmitted by Granada Television. They perform 'Boredom' live in the studio. In the week following the broadcast, Shelley has his unemployment benefit of £10.56 stopped. Actor Albert Finney, who is also appearing on the programme compliments the band on their sound. Granada Television have no record of this appearance in the archives library.

Tues 12th
Buzzcocks play The Oaks, Barlow Moor Road, Chorlton, south Manchester. This tiny stage also played host to Johnny Thunders and the original line-up of Siouxsie And The Banshee's.

Thurs 14th
Desperate to find gigs, Buzzcocks support Manchester band Sad Cafe in a one-off gig at Blackburn's Golden Palms. Buzzcocks play 'Breakdown/Fast Cars/Boredom/Times Up/Friends Of Mine/No Reply/What Do I Get?/Sixteen Again' and encore with 'Love Battery'. Keith Wilde, formerly of Kogg, joins the band's sound crew.

May
Sun 1st
The Clash's headline 'White Riot' tour opens at Guildford, Civic Hall with Buzzcocks, Subway Sect and The Slits as supporting acts. After the troubles experienced by the infamous 'Anarchy In The UK' tour, these dates represented the first proper punk road show. (For the following tour dates, ** denotes 'White Riot' tour, where Buzzcocks are *not* the headlining band).

Mon 2nd
Buzzcocks play Band On The Wall, a gig advertised by a Malcolm Garrett designed poster featuring the Buzzcocks' official logo for the first time. Shelley sings with an inflated condom attached to his microphone stand. The band are joined onstage for the encore by Howard Devoto, who yells that he is "dusting off his hat". Tonight, 'Jon The Postman' makes his debut appearance with the band. Jon was the original Buzzcocks fan, who had attended their very first gig at Lesser Free Trade Hall, and proceeded to travel to all their shows until April 1978. At this show, as with all ensuing appearances, Jon would always make it onto the stage before the show ended. Once there, he would promptly launch into his rendition of 'Louie, Louie', usually with a bottle of Newcastle Brown Ale in his hand, and would be joined onstage for the chorus by the audience and the band themselves. His celebrity grew such that at his final night at The Electric Circus, Shelley introduced him thus: "That's it from us, but the favourite of all Manchester, the one guy who never appears on the bill but is always there - Jon The Postman, step forward, this is your life!"

Meanwhile, the 'White Riot' tour plays Chester, Rascals.

Tues 3rd   Birmingham, Barbarella's (**)

Wed 4th   Swindon, The Affair (**)

Thurs 5th   Liverpool, Eric's (**)

Fri 6th   Aberdeen University (**)

Sat 7th   Edinburgh, Playhouse Theatre (**)

Sun 8th   Manchester, Electric Circus (**)

Mon 9th   London, Rainbow Theatre (**)
The Jam are added to the line-up for tonight's billing only.

Tues 10th   Kidderminster, Town Hall (**)
Cancelled as Mick Jones of The Clash has an operation on his finger.

Thurs 12th   Nottingham, Palais (**) Cancelled - see above.

Fri 13th   Buzzcocks play Parr Hall in Warrington, supporting The Heartbreakers. Manchester band Slaughter And The Dogs are also on the bill, as are The Spitfire Boys.

The 'White Riot' tour concert at Leicester is cancelled.

Sat 14th
NME announce that Devoto is contemplating releasing an EP of spoken word excerpts from the writings of Samuel Beckett on the New Hormones label, which by now was already encompassing far more ideas than just record releases.

Sun 15th   Plymouth, Fiesta (**)

Mon 16th   Swansea, University (**)

Tues 17th   Leeds, Polytechnic (**)

Thurs 19th   Middlesborough, Rock Garden (**)

Fri 20th   Newcastle, University (**)

Sat 21st   St. Albans, City Hall (**)

Sun 22nd   Maidenhead, Skindles (**) - cancelled

Mon 23rd   Stafford, Top of the World (**)

Tues 24th   Cardiff, Top Rank (**)

Wed 25th   Brighton, Polytechnic (**)

Thurs 26th   Bristol, Colston Hall (**)

Fri 27th   West Runton, The Pavillion (**)

Sat 28th   Canterbury, Odeon (**)

Sun 29th
Buzzcocks play Manchester, Electric Circus with support Penetration and Warsaw. Warsaw are originally billed as Stiff Kittens, a name

given to them by Shelley, but on the night they change the band title. Later, they change it once more to Joy Division. It is an excellent gig, although during the encore, Shelley's amp packs up mid-way through 'Boredom'. Shelley wears a mock-leopard skin sleeve-less top.

Andrew Lauder of United Artists comes up from London to see the band for the first time: "I remember I had made my mind up to sign them even before I had seen them. What I remember most is that after the gig I phoned a cab to take me back to my hotel, because I didn't like the thought of walking round Collyhurst at midnight."

Meanwhile, the 'White Riot' tour play Chelmsford, Chancellor Hall.

Mon 30th
'White Riot' tour ends at Dunstable, California Ballroom (**).

June
Fri 3rd
Pete Shelley is interviewed backstage at the Electric Circus by Paul Morley for the *New Manchester Review* magazine, and then photographed by Kevin Cummins.

Sun 5th   Aberdeen, Music Hall (cancelled)

Fri 10th
The Roxy, London WC2 live compilation album is released on EMI's Harvest label. The album was recorded between January and April 1977 and features tracks from Buzzcocks, Slaughter And The Dogs, The Unwanted, The Adverts, Wire, X-Ray Spex, Eater and Johnny Moped. Buzzcocks tracks are 'Love Battery' and 'Breakdown'.

Sat 18th
Buzzcocks gig at Electric Circus the previous Sunday is reviewed in the *NME* by Paul Morley.

Fri 24th
Buzzcocks gig at Colwyn Bay, Pavillion is cancelled as a direct result of a 'punk backlash' by many venue owners up and down the country.

Sat 25th
Buzzcocks play N.E. London Polytechnic (for 'Rock Against Racism') with support The Verbals.

July
Sat 2nd
Adverts for *The Roxy, London WC2* compilation album appear in the music press.

Mon 4th
Buzzcocks play The Vortex, London with fellow Manchester band, The Fall and John Cooper-Clarke. During the sound check, earlier in the afternoon, Howard Devoto is photographed on vocals with the band by Kevin Cummins. On the night, Johnny Thunders And The Heartbreakers turn up asking to play a couple of numbers since it is American Independence Day. Buzzcocks are initially reluctant but eventually agree. However, Buzzcocks' roadie Eric Ramsden is so pissed off he nails Johnny Thunders' leather jacket to the dressing room floor.

Fri 8th
BBC Television film crews are on location in Manchester (8th, 10th, 11th and 12th July) filming for a BBC 2 *Brass Tacks* special on punk in that city. They interview original Manchester punks Allan and Linda Deaves, Paul Doyle, Denise Lloyd and, amongst others, Pete Shelley.

Sun 10th
A gig at the Electric Circus featuring The Vibrators, The Drones and Penetration is filmed for *Brass Tacks*, and members of the audience are also interviewed. Shelley asks reporter Eric Robson "Do I look vile and obscene?"

Mon 25th   Doncaster, Outlook Club

Wed 27th   Westcliffe-on-Sea, Queens Hotel

August
Tues 2nd   Manchester, Electric Circus

Wed 3rd
The *Brass Tacks* special on punk is screened. Presenter Brian Trueman

48

speaks to councillors representing the various area's that have banned punk. A studio debate featuring John Peel, Ian Hodge (from The Worst) and Pete Shelley defend the punk movement, whilst Pastor John Cooper, who banned punk in Caerphilly, talks of the violence that it attracts.

Thurs 4th
Buzzcocks play London's Marquee Club with support band Wire. The show breaks the Marquee attendance record.

Fri 5th
Back in Manchester, Shelley and a friend, Franny Taylor, are walking for a bus after a night at The Ranch Club, when they are attacked by a group of men in Picadilly Gardens. Although shaken, neither are badly hurt.

Tues 16th
Buzzcocks play Electric Circus, where admission is free. In Memphis, Elvis Aaron Presley is found dead. The preceding week, Richard Boon had received several phone-calls offering the band record deals, including a very strong offer from Maurice Oberstein of CBS on the morning of this gig. However, Andrew Lauder of United Artists has beaten them all to the band's signatures, and so at the bar of The Electric Circus following the show, Buzzcocks sign the deal, worth £75,000 for the first two years.

Granada Television film the Buzzcocks' performance, and footage of the band performing 'What Do I Get?' is included in the 'So It Goes' programme screened on October 9th.

Peter Jones, known among many fans as 'Mr. Buzzcocks' sees the band for the first time.

Fri 19th
Buzzcocks, Boon and most of the crew set out in a van for Wolverhampton's Lafayette club to see a band advertised as The Spots, but who are actually the Sex Pistols on a secret tour.

Sat 20th   Droitwich Punk Festival (cancelled)
Sounds report that as part of the 'Summer In The City' season of films at The Other Cinema, Tottenham Street, London, scheduled for

August 21st, there will be film of The Clash, Squeeze and Buzzcocks on stage.

Sat 23rd
Under an official contract drawn up by the band's solicitors, Richard Boon is officially recognised as manager of Buzzcocks.

Buzzcocks record a session for Manchester's Picadilly Radio. They record 'What Ever Happened To?/What Do I Get?/Orgasm Addict' and 'Oh Shit!'.

Thurs 25th
Buzzcocks play Leeds Polytechnic. Innocently, Shelley wears a Manchester United football shirt onstage. To the Leeds United fans present, this is highly provocative, and as they taunt the band, a drunken Davies invites members of the audience onstage to "have a go". After only a couple of numbers, Shelley announces: "Someone over there's just spat, we're off!" Outside, the band make a speedy exit to their car, whose back window is smashed as they drive off. This was one of many outbursts Davies made onstage, and he proved to be something of a loose cannon. Shelley himself later said of him that "he was a law unto himself on the stage." Tonight is also the last time Shelley uses his broken 'Starway' guitar, which is later given to his younger brother Gary.

Three numbers from the Leeds Polytechnic gig and Davies' outburst are included on the bootleg album *Razor Cut*, released in 1979.

Tues 30th-Wed 31st
Buzzcocks are recording their first demo's for UA at Indigo Studios in Manchester with Martin Rushent, who has produced, amongst others, Shirley Bassey as well as The Groundhogs - when he first heard 'Spiral Scratch' he told Andrew Lauder: "If you sign them, I'll produce them." Tracks recorded are 'Orgasm Addict/What Do I Get?/No Reply' and 'What Ever Happened To?' Two songs from the session tape also appear on the bootleg album *Razor Cut*.

September
Thurs 1st
Buzzcocks go shopping with the advance they receive from United Artists. One of the conditions of the contract is that part of the

advance must be used to purchase new equipment, so in the weeks that follow, the band purchase a new P.A. system in Watford and a mixing desk from Sigma Systems of Nottingham, while Davies spends over £500 on a new Gibson 'Thunderbird' bass guitar.

A newly equipped Buzzcocks play Manchester, Rafters Club with support The Prefects. The club itself is situated in the basement of Fagin's Night Club in the city centre, and would host many punk and rock gigs from 1977 through to 1979. Tonight, two numbers into the gig, Davies takes his new bass off because he isn't used to it. Shelley uses his new 'Gordon Smith' Gypsy I serial No. 58 for the first time - unfortunately, this is stolen some month's later.

19 year old Prestwich punk Steve Garvey is in the audience, this being the second time he has seen the band with Davies on bass guitar. He tells his friends "I'm going to be in this band!"

Fri 2nd
Buzzcocks meet at 11.00am in Manchester's Picadilly Hotel for breakfast, at the expense of their record company. As breakfasts are off, Shelley settles for a beer in the lounge instead. The band are then interviewed by Caroline Coon for *Sounds*.

Sat 3rd   Liverpool, Eric's

Sun 4th
Buzzcocks play The Greyhound in Croydon. This booking was originally made for London's Sundown Club, but due to renovations lasting four weeks, all gigs are transferred to the Croydon venue. Francis Taylor helps to organise a coach party of Manchester fans down to the gig. United Artists' Andrew Lauder and Martin Rushent both attend the gig.

Buzzcocks perform 'Moving Away From The Pulsebeat' for the first time ever live.

Tues 6th
Buzzcocks play Barbarella's in Birmingham, with The Worst and The Fall supporting. One fan describes the gig as "the definitive Buzzcocks live performance, the best I ever saw."

Wed 7th
Buzzcocks are at Maida Vale, Studio 4, recording three tracks for the *John Peel Show* to be broadcast on September 19th. The tracks are 'Fast Cars/Moving Away From The Pulsebeat/What Do I Get?'. The band receive a payment of £62 for the session from the BBC.

Fri 9th
Buzzcocks are at T.W. Studios, Fulham to begin recording their debut single for United Artists with producer Martin Rushent. They record 'What Do I Get?/Orgasm Addict/Oh Shit!/What Ever Happened To?' Two other tracks also recorded are different takes of 'Orgasm Addict' and 'What Ever Happened To?'.

Sat 10th
A review of the previous week's Buzzcocks concert at Rafters is featured in *Record Mirror*.

Sat 17th
An interview with Buzzcocks (including Davies - one of only two features he appeared in) is featured in *Record Mirror*. A two-page interview, with photographs, appears in *Sounds*. A review of the Greyhound gig is also featured. Reviewer Chas de Whalley comments "a mountain-like Davies on bass looks like he could take on a whole hall full of Teds with one hand behind his back!"

Mon 19th
John Peel Show broadcasts the Buzzcocks session recorded on September 7th.

Wed 21st
Buzzcocks are at Olympic Studios, Barnes, recording demo's for their debut single. After a heated argument with Shelley, Davies throws his brand new Gibson bass down a flight of stairs.

Sat 24th
Pete Shelley moves into 16, Pinnington Road, Gorton, Manchester paying £14.88 per week.

Wed 28th
Buzzcocks are photographed in a Manchester bus shelter for the

sleeve of their debut single 'Orgasm Addict' by Kevin Cummins. Individual shots are also taken against a backdrop of corrugated sheeting and are later used by the fan-club for badges.

October
Sat 1st
A detailed two page interview with photographs is featured in *Zig Zag* magazine.

First of a two-night 'closure gig' at Electric Circus. Although Buzzcocks do not play, a host of other quality Manchester acts do. Making a one-off appearance are The Negatives, lead by *NME* columnist Paul Morley. Buzzcocks' manager Richard Boon plays saxophone, and photographer Kevin Cummins plays drums.

Sun 2nd
Second night of the Electric Circus closure gig. Buzzcocks play 'Fast Cars/Boredom/Sixteen/You Tear Me Up/Orgasm Addict/Moving Away From The Pulsebeat/Love Battery/Times Up' and a debut live version of 'Fiction Romance'. The band encore with 'Louie Louie' before being joined on-stage by Jon The Postman and a section of the audience.

Meanwhile, Howard Devoto has formed a new band called Magazine. Devoto met guitarist John McGeoch in April 1977, and during the summer recruited Bob Dickinson on keyboards, Barry Adamson on bass and Martin Jackson on drums. Tonight, Magazine make a guest appearance before Devoto's former band, playing three songs only, 'The Light Pours Out Of Me/Shot By Both Sides/I Love You, You Big Dummy'. They use equipment borrowed from Buzzcocks.

Virgin Records record the weekend for a forthcoming compilation album, but only one Buzzcocks track appears, 'Times Up'. However, a mixing desk recording of the entire Buzzcocks set features on the bootleg album *Best In Good Food*, released in May 1978.

Mon 3rd
Buzzcocks play Blackpool's Jenkinson's with support band The Prefects.

Tues 4th
Buzzcocks play London's Marquee Club with support Adam and the Ants featuring Jordan.

Fri 7th   Liverpool, Polytechnic

Sat 8th
Buzzcocks play Mr. Georges in Coventry. Davies and Eric Ramsden had been drinking all afternoon and shortly after the gig has started Davies takes off his beloved Gibson bass, smashes it against the equipment and walks off. Shelley simply tells Diggle to turn up the bass on his amplifier and the band finish the set without him. After a heated argument, Davies travels back to Manchester in the back of the crew van. After a series of such incidents, and with band tension mounting, the band make the decision to sack Davies. Buzzcocks' first major headlining tour is days away.

Second series of Granada TV's *So It Goes* series is screened in the London region only, featuring film of Buzzcocks performing 'What Do I Get?' from the Electric Circus on August 16th. Other regions screen the programme the next evening.

Wed 12th
NME reports that "Buzzcocks have sacked their bass player Garth Davies because of "personal and professional incompatibility.""

Thurs 13th
Buzzcocks, minus Davies, are photographed in Manchester by Kevin Cummins.

Sat 15th
Sounds columnist Jon Savage reviews Davies' final gig as "Power Cut At The Electric Circus!"

The *John Peel Show* recording of 'Moving Away From The Pulsebeat' (7th Sept) is featured in Radio 1's *Alan Freeman Show* this afternoon.

Fri 21st
Planned release date for Buzzcocks' debut single release on United Artists, 'Orgasm Addict/What Do I Get?', but due to rehearsals for a new bassist, this is delayed for one week. Arturo Basic of The

Lurkers, Carl Mogg of The Smirks, along with a dozen others are auditioned.

Sat 22nd
Buzzcocks are featured in a *Melody Maker* three page special on the music scene in Manchester.

'Fast Cars', also recorded for the *John Peel Show* (7th Sept), again earns them airtime on the *Alan Freeman Show*.

Mon 24th
Buzzcocks' 'Tour No. 1' is scheduled to open tonight at Swindon, The Affair, in support of their debut release 'Orgasm Addict'. However, because of the on-going auditions the gig is cancelled.

Tues 25th
The Fall are borrowing some of Steve Garvey's equipment to play gigs. They hear of Davies' departure and recommend Garvey to Boon as a replacement. An audition is quickly arranged for that afternoon.

Garvey auditions at Drone Studios, 20 Ellesmere Road, Chorlton, Manchester. His close friend and Fall member, Martin Braham advises him against wearing a leather jacket and bondage trousers. They both go to an Oxfam shop in their hometown of Prestwich, and buy clothes that are "more the Buzzcocks image." Before the audition, Garvey plays along to the 'Spiral Scratch' EP in his bedroom until he knows all four songs. Ironically, Garvey believes his subsequent acceptance into Buzzcocks was "because I bought John Maher a Mars Bar at the corner shop afterwards."

Wed 26th
Due to the auditions, the second night of their 'Tour No. 1' at Burton, 76 Club is also cancelled.

Fri 28th
'Orgasm Addict/What Ever Happened To?' is finally released. Music press advertisements for the single read "Sorry it took so long coming!" and the press themselves were impressed, with *NME* saying "this is one of the sharpest records ever to emerge - do you think Radio 1 will ever play it?" The brilliant punk writer John

Savage later said of the single that "it was the most perfect record of 1977." Unfortunately, any chart potential the single may have had was quickly obliterated by the near universal air play ban slapped on the lead track's suggestive title, playful lyrics and Shelley's mock orgasm. The Linder/Garrett acid yellow sleeve was another classic.

'Orgasm Addict' was oddly inspired by a Christmas job former Buzzcock Devoto had in a Leeds bakery a couple of years before forming the band: "Peter had written the first two lines and the chorus, I wrote the rest of it. I was working in this bakery, and there was somebody there who just stuck these little robins on the Christmas cakes while they were being made."

The flipside 'What Ever Happened To?' featured lyrics credited to Alan Dial (alias Richard Boon), which talked of TV sex, trucks and love.

United Artists send the wrong production master to France making the French release an instant collectors' item, since it features a different take to its UK counterpart.

Howard Devoto and his new band Magazine make their full and official debut tonight at Manchester's Rafter's Club. On the strength of early gigs and Devoto's reputation, Virgin Records sign Magazine and release their debut single, 'Shot By Both Sides/My Mind Ain't So Open' in January 1978.

Sat 29th
Buzzcocks attend The Clash gig at The Apollo in Manchester.

November
Tues 1st
Buzzcocks' 'Tour No. 1' finally opens. With Steve Garvey not quite ready, Buzzcocks use stand-in bassist Barry Adamson for the gig at Maryat Hall in Dundee, with support band The Prefects.

Wed 2nd   Paisley, Disco Harry, same support.

Thurs 3rd   Falkirk, Manique Ballroom, same support.

Fri 4th   Edinburgh, Clouds, same support.

Shelley gets the idea to write 'Ever Fallen In Love (With Someone You Shouldn't've)?' from a line in the Frank Sinatra musical 'Guys and Dolls' which he watches in the Edinburgh hotel lounge where the band are staying. The lead line is inspired by a line from gangster Frank Sinatra's girlfriend, who is eager to tie the knot.

Sun 6th   Stafford, Top of The World with support The Prefects and The Flies.

Mon 7th
Buzzcocks play Buckley, Tivoli Ballroom with support The Flies. The sound check is halted while bingo is played upstairs.

Tues 8th
Buzzcocks shoot their first photo session with the new bassist at Eric's in Liverpool, taken by Kevin Cummins. The same night they attend a Rich Kids' gig, featuring Glen Matlock on bass.

Thurs 10th
Steve Garvey plays his debut gig with Buzzcocks at Nottingham's Sandpiper, a concert originally scheduled for Nottingham, Katies. Supporting are The Lurkers. Soon after joining Buzzcocks, Garvey is nicknamed 'Paddy' by the rest of the band to avoid confusion with Diggle. Both his appearance and his superb bass lines add a new dimension to the band immediately.

Fri 11th   Keele University with support The Lurkers.

Sat 12th   Manchester, Polytechnic, same support.

Sun 13th   Croydon, Greyhound, same support.

Tues 15th   Birmingham, Barbarella's with support The Flies.

Thurs 17th
Buzzcocks are banned from playing Wigan Casino tonight following the intervention of the local police, who announce they will not allow "punk shows of any description" in their town.

Fri 18th   Liverpool, Eric's with support The Fall and The Toilets.

Sat 19th
Ilkley College of Education with support The Worst. When the band arrive, another group insist that they have been booked by the Student's Union as added support. Boon concedes and The Gang of Four play their first ever gig with Buzzcocks, one of many to follow. From hereon, Buzzcocks pursue a policy of offering supports to lesser known bands, such as The Worst, Subway Sect and The Slits, as recognition of the difficulties such groups have securing good gigs.

NME officially reports that Steve Garvey, a 19 year old Mancunian, has joined Buzzcocks as their new bassist.

Sun 20th
Buzzcocks gig at Shrewsbury, Tiffany's is cancelled because their van breaks down at Knutsford Service station.

Mon 21st
London, Marquee Club with support The Flies and The Worst. The band break their own house attendance record. The Clash's Mick Jones attends the gig.

Tues 22nd
Buzzcocks' 'Tour No. 1' ends with a second night at London's Marquee Club with support The Flies.

Wed 23rd
Buzzcocks are photographed by Kevin Cummins at Teddington Motorway Services stop for the front page of *NME*.

Thurs 24th
During another photo session, Kevin Cummins also shoots the band at 'Kitchen Queen' (a major kitchen manufacturers based in Manchester) for the *NME*, after which they travel to Saddleworth Moor for additional shots.

December
Thurs 1st
Buzzcocks are recording demo's for their next single at Olympic Studios, Barnes with Martin Rushent, for rush release. Tracks demo-ed include 'What Do I Get?' and 'Oh Shit!'.

Fri 2nd
Due to these recording commitments, Buzzcocks' concert at Brighton, New Regent is cancelled, and re-scheduled for December 16th.

Sat 3rd
Buzzcocks are recording at Olympic Studios. The *NME* features Buzzcocks on the front cover of a music paper for the first time, and inside an interview and several photographs are spread across two pages.

Sun 4th   Shrewsbury, Tiffany's (cancelled)

Magazine make their television debut on Granada TV's *So It Goes* programme. Also appearing are Nick Lowe, Elvis Costello, The Dave Edmunds Band and John Cooper-Clarke.

Tues 6th
Buzzcocks' 'Tour Number 2' is scheduled to open tonight at Plymouth, Penthouse, but is cancelled as the band are still recording at Olympic.

Wed 7th   Torquay, Town Hall (cancelled)

Thurs 8th   Penzance, The Garden (cancelled).
                Recording for the single is now finished.

Fri 9th
Buzzcocks' 'Tour No. 2' opens at Wolverhampton's Lafayette Club with support Gang of Four.

Sat 10th
Melody Maker feature an interview with Buzzcocks, entitled "Cocks Of The North!"

Sun 11th   London, Roundhouse. Buzzcocks open with a new, instrumental number. The song is the working skeleton for 'I Need', with a melody written by Diggle and which has lyrics added later by Shelley. Other songs performed for the first time are 'I Don't Mind/Get On Our Own/Autonomy'. Special promotional badges for the forthcoming debut album, *Another Music In A Different*

Kitchen, dated 11.12.77, are given out to everyone who attends the gig. Subsequent tours, record releases and special events are each given their own badge, amounting to 28 in total.

Nicky Hamlyn, a friend of Boon's from Art College, shoots 8mm black and white footage of the gig.

Mon 12th   Dewsbury, Pickwick
                         (cancelled due to contractual problems).

Tues 13th   Coventry's Locarno club with support The Guests and The Killjoys, the latter of whom are fronted by Kevin Rowland, later of Dexy's Midnight Runners.

Wed 14th
Buzzcocks are at Morgan Studios in north London recording demo's for the debut album, and therefore cancel tonight's proposed gig at Derby's King's Hall. Songs recorded are 'I Don't Mind/I Need/Fiction Romance/Get On Our Own'.

Thurs 15th
The band take a day off and go to see The Clash at London's Rainbow Theatre.

Fri 16th
Brighton, New Regent with support band Subway Sect. United Artists press office runs a coach full of journalists to the gig from London. This week's issue of *New Manchester Review* features a picture of Shelley captioned "Pete Shelley, teen throb!"

Sun 18th
Manchester, King's Hall, Belle Vue with support bands Siouxsie And The Banshee's and Penetration. The concert is billed as a Christmas party gig, but is marred by fighting in the audience. Again, *Another Music In A Different Kitchen* badges are given out to everyone in the audience, this time dated 18.12.77.

Tues 20th
'Tour No. 2' is scheduled to end tonight at Keighley, Nikkers Club but the show is cancelled.

Fri 23rd
Buzzcocks play Manchester's Ranch Club with supports The Drones, The Nervous Breakdowns and Jon The Postman.

Tues 28th
Buzzcocks begin recording their debut album, *Another Music In A Different Kitchen*, at Olympic Studios with producer Martin Rushent. They record 'Love Battery/No Reply/I Don't Mind/Fast Cars/Get On Our Own/Moving Away From The Pulsebeat'. The band also record the master for the link into 'Boredom'. 'No Reply' is rejected. At this stage, Buzzcocks in the studio are effectively live and consequently highly efficient.

Sat 31st
Andrew Lauder, who joined United Artists in May 1967 when it was called Liberty Records, and was responsible for signing Buzzcocks, leaves the company to form his own label, Radar Records. He is replaced by Tim Chacksfield.

Shelley writes 'Nothing Left' over Christmas 1977.

1978

With all of the important punk groups now signed to major labels, the ideology and direction of punk was increasingly the subject of heated debate. 1978 was the year in which a tangible disenchantment with the new wave started to manifest itself in the growth of other kinds of punk bands, who felt that they represented and expressed its 'real' meaning. At the same time, punk was also becoming a focus for general yobbism, with many gigs being disrupted by boot-boys who weren't interested in the music so much as the chance for a fight.

Sham '69 illustrated these new developments perfectly. Led by the loveable loud-mouth Jimmy Pursey, Sham 69 dealt in beefy, pub-rock punk, with simple football-terrace choruses and lots of street attitude. Robust, banal and a real thrill live, the group attracted a skinhead following from the East End of London who would fight with rival gangs at virtually every gig. Soon, many so-called Oi! bands appeared, taking their lead from Sham and vintage Bethnal Green pubbers Cock Sparrer, whose 'Runnin' Riot' single had featured a photo of a West Ham pitch invasion on its sleeve. Sham's followers thought that punk had sold them a lie. As *Sounds* (and now *Sun*) journalist Garry Bushell said: "People like Joe Strummer were singing about white riots, but living in white mansions." This new kind of street-punk was their revenge.

But Oi! was just one of many turns punk was taking. Industrial and avant-garde groups like Throbbing Gristle were seizing upon the experimental elements within punk and taking them to extremes, while bands such as Wire, XTC, the Slits, Warsaw (an early version of Joy Division) and Magazine (Howard Devoto's new band), were creating jagged art-rock songs which shared all of punk's imagination, but very little of its trademark aggression. Synthesiser bands like Ultravox, Japan and the Human League were also thriving, inspired in part by David Bowie's experimental 1977 electronic album, *Low*.

Yet while this discontentment flourished at an underground level, groups like The Clash, The Jam, the Stranglers and Buzzcocks were easing themselves into the album/tour routine of major label existence. It wasn't all wine and roses, though. Several of their contemporaries weren't equipped to deal with the endless executive meet-and-greets, the lousy tour accommodation and the all-pervading record company bullshit. In February, Johnny Rotten left the Pistols after the last date of their U.S. tour. It had all been too much. Sid was overdosing on heroin left, right and centre, Malcolm McLaren was finding that running a notorious UK punk band was extremely taxing, emotionally and financially, while Cook and Jones just wanted to be in a touring band where they could enjoy free booze and loads of birds. Johnny wanted no part in such a moronic venture. Also struggling to keep afloat were The Damned, who, after officially splitting after their dreadful second album, *Music For Pleasure*, spent much of 1978 toying with the idea of forming punk supergroups and getting drunk. Punk was re-energising itself and running out of steam at the same time, so there was little for a genuinely-talented band like Buzzcocks to do but keep their noses to the grindstone.

Indeed, hard work was paying off. With their fast, melodic punk-pop, Buzzcocks were placed in the forefront of the burgeoning New Wave movement — which basically comprised young punks like the Undertones, The Jam and the Members, plus old Stiff singer-songwriter favourites like Elvis Costello, Wreckless Eric and Lene Lovich, all of whom had little interest in anarchy but a lot of respect for a brilliant and original pop tune. Buzzcocks had, in part, established the blue-print for New Wave pop with their blistering debut album, *Another Music In A Different Kitchen*, issued in January 1978. Throughout the year, they followed it up with a string of classic, three-minute punk songs, all camp innuendo, buzz-saw guitars and nifty choruses other bands would kill for. 'What Do I Get?', 'I Don't Mind', 'Love You More', all hit the charts and burned themselves into the consciousness of a generation. With Devoto no longer around, Shelley's penchant for unashamed pop songs about the cauldron of relationships flourished. Whatever punk was or wasn't, Buzzcocks were proving that they were an inspirational pop force, a fact confirmed by October's critically-acclaimed *Love Bites* LP, which spawned more excellent singles, including of course their greatest success 'Ever Fallen In Love?'.

However, 1978 was to be the last year that punk showed any semblance of unity and adherence to its mythical set of principles that never existed in the first place. Paradoxically, it was also the year that The Jam, The Clash and Buzzcocks released some of the most stunning records of the rock'n'roll era.

January
Thurs 5th
Recording of the Buzzcocks' debut album *Another Music In A Different Kitchen* continues at Olympic Studios, including 'Fiction Romance/Autonomy/Sixteen/I Need/You Tear Me Up/No Reply'.

Sat 7th
Buzzcocks record rough demo's of 'No Reply/Moving Away From The Pulsebeat/Autonomy'.

Sun 8th
Steve Garvey's birthday today, born 1958

Mon 16th
In the morning, the band are at the ITN Studios in Wells Street, London, filming a promotional video featuring 'What Do I Get?' and 'Moving Away From The Pulsebeat'. For the 'Pulsebeat' video, a clear perspex drum kit is hired to accommodate a colour light show. Director Paul Henry, from United Artists' Art Department shoots a clip of the band crashing through a huge white paper background on the set, but this is cut from the finished version.

Tues 17th
Sex Pistols, the band that inspired Howard Devoto and Pete Shelley, split up.

Wed 18th
Buzzcocks and Martin Rushent begin mixing *Another Music In A Different Kitchen* at Olympic.

Fri 20th
The official release date of 'What Do I Get?/Oh Shit!' is put back until February 3rd because of a dispute at EMI Records' pressing plant caused by the profanity of the B-side's title.

Sat 21st
The *NME* 'Thrills' column contains a special feature on this dispute at EMI, whose reason for refusing to press the single is because they find it "offensive". *Melody Maker* report that Buzzcocks have just completed recording their debut album.

Buzzcocks' first rehearsal room, St. Boniface's Church Hall, 1976

Outside St. Boniface's Church Hall

Shelley at Buzzcocks' first gig, Lesser Free Trade Hall, 20/7/76

Lesser Free Trade Hall, 20/7/76

Buzzcocks at the Screen On The Green, 29/7/76

Outside The Screen On The Green (l-r): Howard Devoto, Richard
Boon, John Maher, Phil Diggle, Steve Diggle, Paul Clegg, Pete Shelley

January 29th, 1977

A MERE further mention of punk rock would no doubt bring bellowing yawns from all quarters, as its five minute stint at serious musical acceptance seems long overdue. The elements of punktitude are still apparent within my good degenerate self, however, and I have the impertinence to inform the masses of a quartet infamously known as Buzzcocks who seem to fit so neatly into the punk category, yet have been eschewed from all chances of recognition.

Buzzcocks differ in only one way from their contemporaries: they possess a spark of originality (that was important once, remember?), and their music gives you the impression they spent longer than the customary ten minutes clutching the quill in preparation to write.

Indubitably, Buzzcocks will hardly figure strongly — or even weakly — in the *NME* poll, and in these dark days when Patti Smith, Loudon Wainwright or even the New York Dolls fail to make any impact on Radio One DJs, common sense is therefore not so common. Both this letter and Buzzcocks themselves will probably be filed and forgotten.

But for now, they are only the best kick-ass rock band in the country. Go and see them first and then you may have the audacity to contradict me, you stupid sluts.
STEVE MORRISSEY, Stretford, Manchester.

Howard Devoto, 1976

Leeds Polytechnic, White Riot Tour, 17/5/77

Cardiff Top Rank, White Riot Tour, 24/5/77

Buzzcocks on the road (l-r): manager Richard Boon, roadie Sarge, roadie Eric Ramsden,   John Maher, Steve Diggle, Garth Davies

First promotional shots for United Artists, 2/78

More of first session for United Artists, 2/78

Thurs 26th
To promote the release of 'What Do I Get?', Buzzcocks play a short tour of Ireland. A gig at Queens University in Belfast is cancelled at the last minute due to transport problems.

Fri 27th   Dublin, Trinity College with support The Worst and Dublin band Revolver.

Sat 28th   Cork, Arcadia with support The Worst (cancelled)

Sun 29th   Limerick, Savoy, same support.

February
Thurs 2nd
Money raised at the Electric Circus closure gig (Oct. 2nd 1977) is presented to the Manchester Hospital Scanner Appeal by Shelley and members of The Worst. The cheque bounces.

Fri 3rd
'What Do I Get?/Oh Shit!' is finally released, two weeks late. *Melody Maker* review it strongly, calling it "a masterly single, a superb balance between melodic ingenuity and good old belting power, where the subtle keeps a bracing pace with the exciting. A classic Shelley composition." The public agreed, and Buzzcocks found themselves denting the Top 40 for the first time, reaching the lofty heights of No. 37. At the time of release, 'What Do I Get?' had more impact in the UK punk scene than any other single, except perhaps 'Anarchy In The UK'. This is the first of a series of seven non-LP singles released by the band over the next eighteen months (they are later collected together for the *Singles Going Steady* compilation).

Sat 11th
Diggle buys a second-hand Gibson Les Paul guitar in a Manchester music store. The previous owner was Tony Hicks, guitarist with The Hollies.

Thurs 23rd
Buzzcocks play a warm up gig for Manchester Polytechnic's Gay Society. Shelley premiere's his new two tone green 'What Do I Get?' shirt. The band are interviewed backstage by the *New Manchester Review*.

March

Thurs 2nd

Buzzcocks' 'Tour Number 3', in support of the debut album, opens at Swansea, Circles with The Slits, and also Penetration, who are added on to some dates. The band use their first stage backdrop, made for them by Alastair Brotchie, who also provided the tape of the rising staccato pitch used at the end of the album.

Fri 3rd

Buzzcocks' long-awaited debut LP *Another Music In A Different Kitchen* is released. The photograph used for the sleeve is taken in the kitchen of Olympic Studios, and the twelve tracks are recorded in the same order as the band first wrote and played them. The sleeve is based on a silver and square theme, beginning a continuous trend for subsequent albums. The critical acclaim is immediate and unreserved, fuelled by the momentum gathered by the band's superb opening volley of singles. *Melody Maker* say "An undisputed punk classic, with the Buzzcocks' unique rush of guitar noise. I just want an album unlike any other - what do I get ? One of Britain's best bands!" *Sounds* call it "the clearest and most healthy sign that the Devoto/Shelley chapter is finally closed" whilst *NME* say "With a few minor reservations, the wait has been worth it." The album reached No. 15 in the national listings, reflecting the Buzzcocks' ever growing appeal.

The Daily Mirror 'Pop Club' release balloons from various Virgin stores. Each balloon has a tag and the finder sends the tag away to receive a free copy of the album. Also, a limited number of albums are available in a plastic printed carrier bag. One side reads 'Product', the other a catalogue number.

Buzzcocks' debut album was originally called *A Housewife Choosing Her Own Juices In A Different Kitchen.*

Sat 4th   Woolwich, Thames Polytechnic

NME reviews Buzzcocks' debut album with photographs of the band taken in a Manchester kitchen showroom by Kevin Cummins.

Sun 5th   Hemel Hempstead, Pavillion

Mon 6th   Plymouth, Metro

Tues 7th   Cardiff, Top Rank

Wed 8th   Brighton, Top Rank

Thurs 9th   Portsmouth, Locarno

Fri 10th
In the afternoon the band make a personal appearance at London's
Virgin Records store in Oxford Street. This is the first in a series of
similar appearances, a marketing ploy that set a popular precedent.
On the night, they play London's Lyceum Ballroom with The Slits
and John Cooper-Clarke. The concert is recorded and broadcast by
Capital Radio. 'Breakdown/Fast Cars/Noise Annoys/Moving Away
From The Pulsebeat/Fiction Romance/What Do I Get?/What Ever
Happened To?/Times Up' are featured. Capital Radio destroy the
original multi-track master, but fortunately a 1/4" stereo master
copy is saved by EMI. A complete version of this recording is later
used as part of the box set *Product*.

After the gig, Buzzcocks hold a launch party for their debut album at
The Crown and Anchor, Neal Street, Covent Garden.

Pete Shelley is featured on the front cover of the *New Manchester
Review*, and inside the whole band are interviewed.

Sat 11th   Southampton, University
Buzzcocks gig at Woolwich, (March 4th), is reviewed in the *NME*.

Sun 12th   Chelmsford, Chancellor Hall

Mon 13th
Buzzcocks are at London's famous Abbey Road Studios recording
their new single 'Love You More/Noise Annoys'. They run through
five takes of 'Noise Annoys' and seven takes of 'Love You More'.

Tues 14th   Sheffield, Top Rank

Wed 15th   Bristol, Tiffany's

Thurs 16th   Lancaster University

Fri 17th
In the afternoon the band make a personal appearance at Liverpool's Virgin Records store followed by a concert at Eric's that evening. Tickets for this concert sell out so quickly that another concert has to be arranged in the same venue for March 28th.

Sat 18th
In the afternoon the band make a personal appearance at Leeds' Virgin Records store followed by a concert at the University that evening.

Sun 19th   Coventry, Locarno

Mon 20th   Swindon, The Affair

Tues 21st   Keighley, Nikkers Club (cancelled due to fog on the Pennines)

Wed 22nd
Personal appearance at Newcastle's Virgin Records store followed by a concert at The Mayfair that evening.

Thurs 23rd   Derby, King's Hall

Fri 24th   Birmingham, Top Rank. For some time now, Shelley had noticed one particular fan (Peter Jones) was always in the front row of every single gig. After spotting him in the audience yet again, Shelley calls out and asks him to come early to the following night's concert so that he can meet the band.

Sat 25th   Manchester, Mayflower. Peter Jones meets Buzzcocks for the first time. It transpires that Jones first saw the band at The Electric Circus show when they signed their record deal, and since that night has fanatically travelled from his hometown of Llandudno in Wales to every gig. Hereafter, the band invite him to soundchecks and after-gig parties and he becomes a close friend. Buzzcocks nickname him 'Duds' after his native town, but many fans call him 'Mr. Buzzcocks', such is his dedication. When the band split up in 1981, Jones had seen them play 74 times; following their reformation, by 27/9/93 he had seen them over 150 times, and was duly asked on stage by Shelley to join them and sing the encore of 'Boredom'.

A lengthy three-page article with photographs appears in *Sounds*, entitled "Another Music in a Different Cinema", written by Jane Suck. She has been driven to two concerts by the UA press officer in a hired car for the feature.

Melody Maker take an in-depth look at Buzzcocks' sudden rise to stardom with an article by Ian Birch entitled: "Looking Behind The Buzzcocks Myth."

Sun 26th   Manchester, Mayflower. After the gig a party is held at Shelley's house in Pinnington Road. While the party is going on, the band's Peugeot estate is broken into and Garvey's bass is stolen, along with some luggage.

Mon 27th   Birkenhead, Hamilton Club (cancelled)

Tues 28th   Liverpool, Eric's

Wed 29th   Middleton, Civic Hall

Thurs 30th   Hanley, Victoria Hall. In the afternoon before the gig, the band enjoy a large lunch in an Indian restaurant at the expense of their record company. Diggle is being interviewed by *Zig Zag* magazine.

Fri 31st   Retford, Porterhouse

April
Sun 2nd
Buzzcocks' 'Tour Number 3' ends at The Greyhound in Croydon. John Lydon appears at the rear of the stage during the gig to immense cheers, having just returned from the States. Later, he organises the beers for a small party which is held at Nora Foster's Chelsea house (Foster is the mother of Ari Up of The Slits). Years later, it emerges that Lydon and Foster had secretly been married for some time.

Sat 8th
Sounds report the theft of Garvey's 'Music Man' bass.

Mon 10th
Buzzcocks are at BBC Maida Vale, Studio 4 , recording three tracks for the *John Peel Show*, to be broadcast April 17th. During lunch at the BBC canteen, the band have yet to come up with a title for one of the tracks they have recorded. Shelley thinks of the name 'Doner Kebab' but later changes it to 'Late For The Train'.

Fri 14th
'I Don't Mind/Autonomy' is released, taken from the debut album. Once again the single receives heavy critical acclaim, with the *NME* simply saying it was "the closest the band come to pure pop." Strangely, the single only reached No.55 however.

Mon 17th
BBC Radio broadcast Buzzcocks' second session for the *John Peel Show*. The tracks 'Noise Annoys/Walking Distance/Late For The Train' later appear on the bootleg album *Best In Good Food*.

Wed 26th
Due to the success of the single, the band are invited on to *Top of the Pops* for their debut performance. Since the Musicians' Union does not allow miming to the actual record, the band are sent to Wessex Sound Studio in London to record a BBC 're-make' for the following night's show. In the afternoon the band head for the BBC Television Centre where they record their actual appearance.

Thurs 27th
Buzzcocks' debut *Top of the Pops* appearance is screened. Steve Garvey said of this show "It was always fun to do, it was the most important thing going for pop bands, and I certainly never missed a show as a kid. Plus, the canteen food and drink was cheap, and all subsidised by the taxpayer!"

Sat 29th
'Walking Distance/Noise Annoys/Late For The Train', recorded for the *John Peel Show* (April 10th) are also included on the *Alan Freeman Show*.

May

Fri 5th

Buzzcocks' 'Entertaining Friends' tour opens at Liverpool University with Penetration supporting - these dates were designed to promote both the album and the new single. Shelley's guitar, a Gordon Smith, (serial No. 00053), is stolen from the dressing room.

Sat 6th   Aylesbury, Friars

Mon 8th

Buzzcocks are at BBC Maida Vale, Studio 5, recording three tracks for the the *Kid Jensen Show*, to be broadcast May 29th. During a break in recording, Kim Davies of the *NME* interviews the band in the BBC canteen, then later in a nearby public house.

Tues 9th   Bath, Pavillion

Wed 10th   Cardiff, Top Rank

Fri 12th   Shrewsbury, Tiffany's

Sat 13th

In an interview with *Melody Maker*, Shelley is quoted as saying "Punk is in a decline, it is dead!" A review of Buzzcocks' concert at Aylesbury, Friars (Sat 6th), appears in the *NME*.

Thurs 18th   Newcastle, City Hall

Fri 19th   Bradford, St.George's Hall. A fight breaks out midway through their set when a lone NF supporter starts chanting and is set upon by the crowd. During the fight a man is stabbed. After police arrive, the power to the PA is cut and the band finish the set playing instrumental versions of their best songs, while the audience sing along.

Sat 20th   Bracknell, Sports Centre

Sun 21st   Southampton, Top Rank

Thurs 25th   Middlesborough, Town Hall

Fri 26th   Birmingham, Mayfair

Sat 27th
Buzzcocks are at Advision Studios with Martin Rushent recording mixes of their next single 'Love You More/Noise Annoys'.

Sun 28th   London, Roundhouse with Penetration
and A.T.V. supporting

Mon 29th   London, Roundhouse (cancelled due to noise restrictions imposed by the Greater London Council). BBC Radio broadcast Buzzcocks' session on the *Kid Jensen Show*. Tracks are 'I Don't Mind/Love You More/Noise Annoys'. The session is repeated during the week 12th - 16th June 1978.

June
Thurs 1st   Dublin, Stella (cancelled)

Fri 2nd   Belfast, Ulster Hall (cancelled). Both of these concerts are cancelled due to the ongoing problems with insurance cover in Ireland. The band hope to rearrange the gigs for September.

Sat 3rd
Sounds feature an in-depth look at Buzzcocks' drummer John Maher. The article entitled "From Front Room To Front Line Of The New Wave" concentrates on Maher's choice of equipment and his musical influences, which include Black Sabbath.

Sun 4th   Glasgow, Apollo

Mon 5th   Aberdeen, Music Hall

Tues 6th
Buzzcocks' 'Entertaining Friends' tour ends at Edinburgh's Odeon.

Fri 9th
Shelley meanwhile, has set up a band called The Tiller Boys, featuring himself on guitar, Eric Ramsden on guitar also, and Francis Cookson on drums (Cookson was a friend and flatmate, whose brother Gerard would later become the guitarist with Pete Shelley's solo band). Their music was based around pre-recorded backing

tapes and a drum machine, and offered a rambling electronic set, although in many senses this paved the way for Shelley's later solo work. The band played several local gigs but were heavily criticised in the press. One *Sounds* review said "The Tiller Boys make a big noise, they stand still onstage, to complement the unmoving music - if only they could create an atmosphere then it would be at least satisfying." Tonight, The Tiller Boys play The Factory in Hulme (an old West Indian club originally doing one or two punk nights a month, before Tony Wilson and Alan Erasmus took it over and made The Factory the successor to The Electric Circus as the place to go).

Sun 11th
Buzzcocks are in Birmingham filming for ATV's *Revolver* programme. The band perform 'Love You More' and 'Noise Annoys' live before a packed studio audience, introduced by Peter Cook. Also recording the same day are Nick Lowe, Elvis Costello and Generation X.

Thurs 15th
ITV regions transmit *Revolver* performance.

Sat 17th
Shelley appears on the front page of the *NME*.

Thurs 22nd
Malcolm Garrett finishes a BA Degree in Graphic Design at Manchester Polytechnic.

Fri 30th
The official release date for 'Love You More/Noise Annoys' is delayed until July 7th - the band claim it was the shortest record ever made, and then decide to make it longer.

July
Mon 3rd
Malcolm Garrett joins Andrew Lauder's Radar Records in London as a 'consultant art director'.

Wed 5th
Buzzcocks are again invited on to *Top of the Pops*, to promote their as yet unreleased new single 'Love You More'.

Thurs 6th
'Love You More' is screened on *Top of the Pops*.

Fri 7th
'Love You More/Noise Annoys' is finally and officiaily released. *NME* again lead the critical applause, saying "This is the most realistic sentimental love song ever written." Buzzcocks' reputation for superb singles was strengthening with every release, and their second Top 40 hit was achieved when this release reached No. 34.

Thurs 13th
Rehearsals take place at Manchester's Alexandra Park for Saturday's 'Anti-Nazi League/Rock Against Racism' carnival.

Sat 15th
Buzzcocks play at the Anti-Nazi League festival. Although Buzzcocks are advertised as the headlining band, they insist that Birmingham band Steel Pulse top the bill. Diggle joins Steel Pulse onstage for an encore of their track 'Klu Klux Klan'.

On the same day, all of the Buzzcocks review this week's new releases in *Record Mirror.*

Mon 17th
Buzzcocks are at Arrow Studios in Manchester, already recording demo's for their second album. The band record 'Love Is Lies/Operators Manual/Just Lust/Ever Fallen In Love?/Nothing Left/Sixteen Again/Raison D'Etre/Real World'.

Tues 18th
On a second day at Arrow Studios, they record five more album demo's. The tape operator's writing is so poor that the Two-Inch/24 track tape box is labelled 'Untitled/Illegible'. The tracks are 'Nostalgia/ESP/ Lipstick/Promises/Mother of Turds'.

Fri 21st
Buzzcocks play the scene of their debut gig, the Lesser Free Trade Hall. Howard Devoto joins the band onstage and takes lead vocal on 'I Can't Control Myself' with Steve Diggle on bass. The concert is filmed by Granada TV and segments of the concert are later screened on a Buzzcocks documentary special called *B'dum B'dum..*

Tracks from this gig are later included on the bootleg album *Razor Cuts*, namely 'I Don't Mind/Ever Fallen In Love?/Noise Annoys/Love You More/I Can't Control Myself'.

Thurs 27th
Granada TV transmit *B'dum B'dum*, a 45 minute documentary on both Buzzcocks and the now highly rated Magazine. Shelley's interview is recorded at Woolworth's cafeteria in Picadilly and Devoto's interview is recorded in a luxury box at The Grand Theatre, with both sessions being conducted by Tony Wilson. There is also footage of Buzzcocks' debut gig, with the 8mm footage shot by Mark Roberts.

Sat 29th
Buzzcocks return to Olympic Studios to begin recording their second album *Love Bites*. During the week long session, the band also record the single 'Promises/Lipstick' (the latter was written by Shelley whilst walking back from The Ranch in Manchester, and contained the same riff which Devoto had used for the highly successful 'Shot By Both Sides'). On this day, they take a break from recording and are interviewed in a nearby public house by Kris Needs of *Zig Zag* magazine, whereupon Shelley reveals that he had written 'Operators Manual' after buying a new Hi-fi and thinking how useful it would be if people came with a similar set of instructions. Back in the studio, the band record 'Lipstick/Nostalgia/Walking Distance/Just Lust/Nothing Left/Ever Fallen In Love?/E.S.P.'

Steve Diggle has two songs laid down on demo which are not used 'Jesus Made Me Feel Guilty' and 'The Drive System'. Diggle and Maher also demo a song they have written called 'Mother Of Turds' featuring Diggle on piano. Later in the day, Buzzcocks record 'Promises/Late For The Train/Operators Manual/Real World/ Sixteen Again/Love Is Lies'.

Meanwhile, LWT screen *Revolver* featuring Buzzcocks, Ian Dury And The Blockheads, Siouxsie And The Banshee's and The Vibrators.

Sun 30th
Today the band record additional backing tracks to 'Just Lust/Ever Fallen In Love?/Nothing Left'.

August
Fri 4th
Diggle hires a Gibson acoustic guitar for the continuing sessions. In the afternoon Shelley is interviewed 'live' on Radio 1's *Round Table* show, hosted by Kid Jensen, which focussed on the latest releases. A rehearsal takes place at 5.45pm, and the programme itself is broadcast between 6.00pm and 7.30pm.

Sat 5th
Plans for a free festival at London's Hyde Park with Buzzcocks headlining are cancelled. The promoters could not afford Buzzcocks' expense bill, which was said to be £25,000.

Sun 6th
Buzzcocks finish recording their second album *Love Bites* at Olympic Studios.

Fri 11th
Buzzcocks start the five day mixing of *Love Bites* at Advision Studio in London (Aug 11th-16th).

While the band are mixing *Love Bites*, the rest of The Tiller Boys play support to Gang of Four at York University. The gig, played by Francis Cookson and Eric Ramsden, is recorded and subsequently released on Groovy Records - the off-shoot of The Tiller Boys call themselves Free Agents, and the record is both called, and sells for, £3.33p. Despite Shelley's absence from the live recording, the remaining tracks which make up the album feature Shelley, Cookson and Allan (guitarist/vocalist) with The Worst, recorded at Graveyard Studios in Prestwich, Manchester.

Wed 16th
Buzzcocks finish mixing *Loves Bites* on the first anniversary of their signing to United Artists. The mixing of the future single, 'Promises' and 'Lipstick', is also completed.

Fri 25th
New Hormones, Buzzcocks' own label, set up a fan club with an annual subscription of £1.50. Members receive regular photo's, badges and a newsletter entitled *The Secret Public*.

September
Fri 1st
In the first week of September, Buzzcocks make their first trip to Europe playing five gigs as guests of Blondie on their *Parallel Lines* album tour. Sue Cooper is the band's driver for the dates. Tonight, they play Kerkrade, Holland.

Sat 2nd   Amsterdam, Paradiso.

Mon 4th   Nijmegen, Holland.

Wed 6th   Brussels, Ancienne Belgique.

Thurs 7th   Rotterdam, Eksit.

Fri 8th
'Ever Fallen in Love?/Just Lust' is released, as the first single from the new album. The flipside contains lyrics credited to Alan Dial (alias, Richard Boon), written in a house in Chiswick during the recording of *Love Bites*. Of the lead track, *NME* said "this has all the attributes of a pop classic." The reviewer could not have been more correct - the immediate success was the band's highest chart success, their third Top 40 hit at No.12, and three appearances on *Top of the Pops*; soon after the lead song, with its infectious chorus and wonderful arrangement of minor chords would justifiably earn its own place in pop history as an all time great. Unknown to many, the song was actually written about Shelley's close friend Francis Cookson.

Wed 20th
Buzzcocks record 'Ever Fallen in Love?' at Air Studios for another appearance on *Top of the Pops*, the performance of which is filmed this afternoon.

Thurs 21st
'Ever Fallen In Love?' is screened on *Top of the Pops*. Steve Garvey's Auntie Mavis calls to let him know she is upset that he looked "scruffy on the telly."

Fri 22nd
Buzzcocks complete rehearsals at T.J's in Little Peter Street,

Manchester, before they embark on their album tour, entitled 'Beating Hearts'. T.J's is a disused cotton warehouse whose owner has converted it into rehearsal space for a dozen bands, each renting a room for £25 a week. According to Shelley's watch, they have squeezed 18 songs into 61 minutes.

Love Bites, Buzzcocks' second album, is released, only a lightning fast seven months after their debut long player. The title had originally been pencilled in for the follow-up to their debut 'Spiral Scratch' E.P., prior to signing with United Artists. The eleven track album is presented in a white sleeve with a circular motif, continuing the Garrett theme set by the debut. Once more, the press are highly impressed. *Melody Maker* says "on *Love Bites*, Buzzcocks go a considerable way towards achieving the impossible - by showing how love makes the world go round. Shelley can get away with love songs because of the sharp power of Buzzcocks' rhythm section." *NME* suggest "their prime strength has been their irresistible hook lines. *Love Bites* is full of ringing guitar lines, beautiful minor chords and choruses you simply can't resist singing." *Sounds* went even further, saying "this is Buzzcocks' purest pop move, and yes, it works." *Love Bites* went two places higher than its predecessor and reached No. 13 in the national listings.

Tues 26th
Buzzcocks' soundcrew leave Holyhead harbour at 3.00pm, arriving in Dun Laoghaire, Ireland at 6.30pm.

Wed 27th
The band and manager Boon leave Manchester Airport at 10.15am, arriving in Dublin at 11.00 on flight number EI 205.

Buzzcocks' 'Beating Hearts' tour opens at Dublin's State Cinema with Subway Sect supporting.

Thurs 28th
Buzzcocks travel by train from Dublin to Belfast with Boon. With them on the 11.00am departure from Dublin is *Record Mirror*'s Liam Mackey, who talks to Shelley and Diggle. On their arrival in Belfast, Shelley is interviewed by Downtown Radio. The interview lasts all of three minutes. Tonight, they play Belfast's Ulster Hall.

Fri 29th
The band arrives back in Manchester Airport at 4.50pm.

Sat 30th
An interview with Buzzcocks appears in *Melody Maker*, with accompanying photographs, which took place in a city centre bar. Already, Shelley appears to be growing uncomfortable with the changing face of Buzzcocks - on the album tour dates, Boon has to continually convince the lead singer to stay in the band.

October
Sun 1st   Oxford, New Theatre. The gig climaxes with a gang of about 50 skinheads invading the stage. Earlier fans had repeatedly jumped on stage and were pushed off by bouncers, prompting Shelley to announce that the security were employed by the theatre and not the band: "We can't control them!" he shouts.

Mon 2nd   Leicester, De Montford Hall

Tues 3rd   Norwich, St. Andrew's Hall

Wed 4th   Chelmsford, The Odeon. The band are interviewed by the *Essex Chronicle* and the *Chelmsford Weekly News*.

Thurs 5th
As 'Ever Fallen in Love?' enters the Top 30, their appearance on *Top of the Pops* is repeated. Tonight, the band play Middleton, Civic Hall

Sat 7th   Liverpool, The Empire. Garvey has his shirt ripped off by female fans outside the venue.

Sun 8th   Birmingham, The Odeon

Mon 9th   Swansea, Top Rank

Tues 10th   Cardiff, Top Rank

Wed 11th   Taunton, The Odeon

Fri 13th   Plymouth, Top Rank

Sat 14th   Torquay, Town Hall. Meanwhile, Buzzcocks appear on the front cover of *Record Mirror*, and inside the feature tells of their recent tour of Ireland.

Sun 15th   Sheffield, Top Rank

Mon 16th   Hanley, Victoria Hall

Tues 17th
The band and crew stay at the International Hotel, in order to be at the BBC Maida Vale Studio for 9.30am the following morning.

Wed 18th
Buzzcocks are at Maida Vale, Studio 4, recording four tracks for the *John Peel Show*, to be broadcast October 23rd. The tracks are 'Promises/Lipstick/Everybody's Happy Nowadays/ Sixteen Again'.

Thurs 19th
'Ever Fallen in Love?' reaches Number 12 in the charts and *Top of the Pops* screen their performance again. Tonight, they play Malvern, Winter Garden.

Fri 20th   Blackpool, Tiffany's

Sat 21st   Glasgow, Apollo Theatre. A review of the previous week's gig at Sheffield Top Rank appears in the *NME*.

Sun 22nd   Aberdeen, Capital

Mon 23rd   Edinburgh, The Odeon. John Peel session from 18th October is broadcast.

Tues 24th   Newcastle, City Hall

Thurs 26th   Bradford, St. George's Hall

Fri 27th   Manchester, Apollo Theatre. The gig is recorded by United Artists and mixed at Advision Studio by Martin Rushent.

Sat 28th   Derby, King's Hall

Sun 29th   Coventry, Theatre

Mon 30th   Bristol, Colston Hall. The endless touring has left Shelley in a frail state, and he has been feeling increasingly creatively trapped within a band who are expected to release only three minute pop songs. He is desperately unhappy and physically very low. His musical parameters have been expanding constantly, and he is fascinated by the possibilities offered by electronic music, and would like to experiment with other projects, such as The Tiller Boys. By this gig, the strain finally surfaces. Not for the first time on these dates, Shelley locks himself in his hotel room before the gig and tells tour manager Pete Monks he is leaving the band. Boon persuades him otherwise.

Tues 31st   Portsmouth, Guild Hall

November
Wed 1st   Bath, University

Fri 3rd   Canterbury, The Odeon

Sat 4th   London, Hammersmith Odeon

Mon 6th   Hemel Hempstead, The Pavillion

Tues 7th   Bournemouth, Winter Garden

Wed 8th   Brighton, Top Rank. The sold out show of 2000 people erupts into riot at the end of the set when bottles and cans are thrown onstage. The violence escalates as fans invade the stage and in the process Maher's drum kit is smashed, Shelley's amp is stolen, Garvey's bass amp is damaged and two other amps are thrown off the stage. Some observers feel it is the band's refusal to play an encore that triggers the mayhem. The total cost of the damage is estimated at £1,500. Immediately after the show has finished, Brighton police intercept four people carrying stolen equipment from the venue.

Thurs 9th   Guildford, Civic Hall.
            The Undertones are in the audience.

Sat 11th
NME begins a review of the concert at the Hammersmith Odeon with "After just two years, Buzzcocks have shot to the top!"

Sun 12th
Buzzcocks' 'Beating Hearts' tour end at the Manchester Apollo.

Tues 14th
Buzzcocks are at BBC Television Centre, Shepherds Bush, to record a live performance for tonight's *Old Grey Whistle Test*. The band perform 'Sixteen Again' and 'Nothing Left', which is screened later that same evening and repeated on Saturday 18th November.

Wed 15th
Buzzcocks are at the BBC Television Centre recording an appearance on *Top of the Pops* to promote their forthcoming single 'Promises'.

Thurs 16th
Buzzcocks are at the BBC Playhouse Theatre in Manchester recording three tracks for the the *Kid Jensen Show*. The tracks are 'Sixteen Again/What Do I Get?/Promises', and are broadcast throughout the week 4th - 8th December and repeated 11th - 15th December 1978. Buzzcocks' performance of 'Promises' for *Top of the Pops* is screened.

Fri 17th
'Promises/Lipstick' is released, the band's seventh single since their formation. The public and media had now come to expect phenomenal singles from the Buzzcocks, and with this track they continued the incredibly high standard, with *Melody Maker* observing "a crisp intro leading into a steely rhythm drive - nothing new, but the standard is as high as ever."

To promote the new single, Buzzcocks make a video at a community centre in Manchester. A similar promo is also shot for 'Lipstick' at nearby Arrow Studios. The result of the continued profile and acclaim was yet another Top 40 hit, their fourth, at No. 20.

Sat 18th
A letter from Steve Diggle appears in the *NME* explaining the cause of the riot at the Brighton Top Rank concert.

Sat 25th
A series of letters attacking Buzzcocks, written by Brighton 'mods', appear in *Sounds*.

Thurs 30th
Top of the Pops screens Buzzcocks' promo for 'Promises'.

December
Sat 2nd
NME 'Thrills' column interviews Shelley with a heading that reads "Why I Never Comb My Hair!"

Mon 4th
The Playhouse Theatre session, recorded for the *Kid Jensen Show* is broadcast on the *Tony Blackburn Show* throughout this week, and again from 11th - 15th December.

Thurs 14th
Top of the Pops screens a repeat of 'Promises' video, which continues to climb the charts.

Sat 23rd
In the *NME* 'Vinyl Finals', Buzzcocks' 'Ever Fallen In Love?' is voted No.1 Single Of The Year, 'What Do I Get?' comes in at No. 19 and, in the album section, their debut long player *Another Music In A Different Kitchen* is at No.25.

1979-1981

By 1979, punk in its purest form was dead. Pete Shelley had said so himself in the early summer of 1978. The Pistols had split a year earlier in America, with Rotten flying home to form the experimental anti-rock band Public Image Limited. (Interviewed about the split, Rotten said "This is not the death of punk rock, it is the demise of one band. It stopped the rise of The Rolling Stones in the 80's ever happening"). The Clash's second album, *Give 'Em Enough Rope*, had proved to be an American-orientated FM rock affair, layered with full-on lead-guitar breaks and stunted by a sluggish production from Blue Oyster Cult producer Sandy Pearlman. The Damned had reformed, and were working on a progressive opus called Machine Gun Etiquette, while The Jam had cut their best LP, the blistering *All Mod Cons*, by reviving the vintage '60s sounds of The Who, The Kinks and The Beatles. With the Vibrators turning into a cartoon punk band, Siouxsie struggling with line-up changes and Generation X flailing about on their last legs, only Buzzcocks seemed to be offering a forward-looking version of what they'd been doing back in '76.

However, although the hits kept coming — 'Promises', 'Everybody's Happy Nowadays', 'Harmony In My Head' — behind the scenes in the Buzzcocks' camp, the divergent ideas that were reshaping the overall sounds of other punk groups were being quietly suppressed. The inevitable result was tension. In January 1979, Steve Garvey began moonlighting with another Manchester group, the Teardrops, while John Maher worked on an album with self-styled punk poet Patrick Fitzgerald. The following month Pete Shelley took time off, playing acoustic sets of material the band couldn't accommodate within their set. The future looked very shaky indeed — so much so that Steve Diggle was compelled to deny in public that the band were splitting. In addition, the continuing backlash against punk affected Buzzcocks as well, despite their having distanced themselves from the movement at every opportunity.

Yet a prevailing desire to move on and away from punk was evident everywhere you looked. In the summer of 1979, the Two Tone phenomena exploded, prompting hundreds of bands previously toying with punk to try their hands at ska and reggae. All of a sudden punk looked old, even though New Wave acts like the Undertones, who were still finding their feet, were still criminally young. By October, the Specials, Madness, the Beat and the Selecter were being joined in their revivalism by an army of Mod outfits, who saw The Jam as the new messiahs, and elected Paul Weller their unofficial — and reluctant — spokesman.

To a certain extent, Buzzcocks remained impervious to these upheavals. Like The Clash, they spent the autumn trying to crack America, before returning home to promote their third and arguably best LP, *A Different Kind Of Tension*, a quirkier and more incisive work than its two predecessors.

As a new decade dawned, punk was now firmly a thing of the past, a fact underscored by the release on 7th December 1979 of The Clash's *London Calling*, a sprawling, inspirational brew of rock'n'roll, reggae, ska, rock and funk, which recast the group in their original role of musical pioneers and hip-shooting renegades. Aware that the '80s would demand something new of them, Buzzcocks retreated into the studio, where they worked on new material featuring brass and string arrangements. However, all was not well: between the sessions, all four members took time out for solo ventures, with John Maher even joining the Things permanently on drums (though still remaining loyal to his Buzzcocks commitments). Over the next few months, the very difficult fourth album gradually took shape, though their record company — who'd recently been taken over by EMI — were proving less supportive than the band hoped. Even so, the band maintained a positive attitude, regularly playing live throughout the year, and releasing the robust and catchy double-A-side, 'Are Everything/Why She's A Girl From The Chainstore' in late summer.

But despite a flurry of activity towards the end of the year, including tours of Britain and the States, the fourth album failed to materialise, and matters worsened in early 1981 when recording ground to a halt because of record company disinterest. Buzzcocks were drifting apart — Diggle, Garvey and Maher were all involved in side projects, while a solo career became an increasingly attractive prospect for Pete Shelley, whose boredom with his previous format had dragged him into the depths of despair. So much so, in fact, that in February 1981, Shelley began to work with producer Martin Rushent without the other members present. By the following month, he'd quit. Buzzcocks were dead.

January

Mon 1st
Buzzcocks are at Strawberry Studios, Stockport with Martin Rushent rehearsing and demo-ing their next single, 'Everybody's Happy Nowadays/Why Can't I Touch It?'

Tues 9th
Kevin Cummins takes pictures of the band whilst they rehearse at T.J's.

Thurs 11th
At this point, various members of Buzzcocks begin to be involved in several solo projects, which provided a useful break from the intense touring schedules of their main band. Despite inevitable rumours that were soon circulated about a Buzzcocks split, in actual fact at this stage, the solo activities were nothing more than a few dates and minor recording sessions.

Buzzcocks play Manchester Polytechnic in aid of local charity Shades with Teardrops supporting. The gig is described as 'The Annual Polytechnic Word of Mouth Charity Gig', and despite the fact it is unadvertised and there is no public transport in the city due to a petrol shortage, Buzzcocks still attract a full house and raise £500 for the charity.

Fri 12th
The Teardrops, featuring Buzzcocks' bassist Steve Garvey and ex-members of The Fall, play Manchester's Russell Club. *Sounds* carry an exclusive story of the release of a single by this new band whose line-up also features ex-Fall drummer Karl Burns.

Sat 20th
Diggle and Maher are rehearsing at T.J's., while Garvey is recording demo's at Cargo Studio, in Rochdale. BBC Radio broadcast more tracks from the Playhouse Theatre sessions, this time on the *Mike Read Show*.

Thurs 25th- Fri 26th   Buzzcocks rehearsing at T.J's.

Sat 27th-Sun 28th
With the demo's complete, Buzzcocks are now back at Strawberry

Studios with Martin Rushent, to record the new single, 'Everybody's Happy Nowadays/Why Can't I Touch It?'.

Mon 29th
Maher is at Matrix Studios, Little Russell Street, London recording material with Patrick Fitzgerald, for the latter's debut album *Grubby Stories*.

February
Sat 10th
Amid mounting speculation, a *Melody Maker* news items reads "Buzzcocks - No Splits, Just Solo's!" containing a statement from Steve Diggle which says "This solo activity does not mean we're splitting up. It means we're going to be twice as busy as usual and our manager is losing his hair."

Fri 16th
Peter Campbell McNeish changes his name officially by deed poll to Pete Shelley.

Sat 24th
Sounds report that Shelley is in the studio with Albertos Y Lost Trios Paranoias producing a number of tracks for them.

Sun 25th
Manchester's Picadilly Radio commence broadcast of a solo accoustic guitar session by Shelley on a one-a-night basis. The tracks recorded include 'Maxine/I Don't Know What It Is/Homosapien'.

Wed 28th
Buzzcocks' crew leave Dover on the 7.10pm ferry arriving in Ostende at 11.40pm, in preparation for the band's first European headlining tour. The band have arrived in London from Manchester and in the afternoon they are at Eden Studios recording 'Everybody's Happy Nowadays' for a scheduled appearance on *Top of the Pops*. These European dates are designed to promote the new single - along the way they appear on two television shows and play to packed audiences most nights. Subsequent sales in Germany and Sweden are very high. Also on these dates, Buzzcocks' excess accelerates, with the band staying in expensive hotels, drinking champagne most nights and smugly beginning to distance

themselves from their fans. The original spirit appeared to be getting swamped by the bloated expense account.

Thurs 29th
Tim Lyon forms The Things, who will go on to support Buzzcocks and feature Maher on drums.

March
Thurs 1st
Buzzcocks arrive in Brussels at 11.50am for the opening date of the European Tour at Liege, Centre Culturel de Chenee, with Gang of Four supporting.

Fri 2nd   Amsterdam, Paradiso Club. The gig is recorded by Vara Radio and the band are interviewed at the Amsterdam Crest Hotel. Back at home, 'Everybody's Happy Nowadays' is released. Of this record, *Melody Maker* said "this is an absurdly catchy and subtly sardonic release." The irony of the title was lost on most - Shelley's depression and the stress that was mounting within the band began to hurtle out of control.

Sat 3rd   Rotterdam, Exit Club

Mon 5th
Buzzcocks arrive at RTBF Studio 6 for a Belgian TV Special called *Follies* the following day, which also features The Jam. The band rehearse from 1.30pm until 6.00pm.

Tues 6th
Buzzcocks play live for *Follies*, filmed in front of a live audience and featuring 30 minutes of material from the band. The band spend the night at the Queen Ann hotel where they are besieged by the popular Belgian music press - throughout this tour their press schedules are hectic and ceaseless.

Wed 7th
Buzzcocks arrive in Paris at 12.20pm, and spend the day doing photo sessions or interviews.

Thurs 8th
Zurich, Volkshaus (cancelled). Instead the band fly to Munich

Airport where in the afternoon they are filmed for the German music programme *Rock Pop* miming 'Everybody's Happy Nowadays'.

Back at home, Buzzcocks' pre-recorded 'Everybody's Happy Nowadays' is screened on *Top of the Pops*. While the band perform, Shelley has £8 in notes showing from the breast pocket of his garish flock jacket, about which he later said "money is a fashion accessory". It was a bizarre drunken performance.

Sat 10th   Berlin, Kant Kino.

Sun 11th   Hamburg, Markethalle. BBC Radio broadcast tracks from a pre-recorded session by Buzzcocks on the *Paul Burnett Show* throughout the week 12th - 16th March and repeated 19th - 23rd March 1979.

Tues 13th
Press conference in the Zhivago Restaurant, followed by a gig at Club 7 in Oslo. Before the gig, the road crew are detained by customs, strip searched and the equipment dismantled. They are released with barely enough time to get the gig on the road.

Wed 14th   Gothenburg, Club 14. This club is on the fourth floor, and the crew are faced with having to move the entire contents of a 40 foot truck up a narrow flight of stairs with only two teenage boys to help. The gig is cancelled.

Thurs 15th   Stockholm, Domino Club.

Sat 17th
Buzzcocks make an appearance on Swedish TV followed by a personal appearance at a Swedish record store. The evening's concert is at Barbarella's in Vaxjo.

At home, Buzzcocks are featured in colour on the front cover of *Record Mirror*, with a full interview inside.

Sun 18th
Buzzcocks arrive back in Manchester. While they are away Shelley has some albums stolen from his home, but cannot understand why both his copies of the bootleg album *Times Up* are not taken.

Mon 19th   Helsinki, House of Culture (cancelled)

Thurs 22nd
'Everybody's Happy Nowadays' has entered the Top Thirty at No. 29, (their fifth Top 40 hit) so *Top of the Pops* screen another repeat of the band's performance.

Fri 23rd
Shelley is at New Hormones office reading fan mail and is joined later by Garvey. They meet the rest of the band at the huge King's Hall venue at Belle Vue, Manchester for a soundcheck. It is here that the band's 'UK Mini Tour' is to open tonight with Ludus supporting, a band fronted by Linder, Buzzcocks' erstwhile visual collaborator.

Sat 24th   Carlisle, Market Hall

Sun 25th   Blackburn, King George's Hall. The band threaten to leave the stage because so many objects are being thrown at them by the audience.

Mon 26th   Peterborough, Wirrana Stadium. With an insurgence of fascist violence throughout the UK, focussing predominantly at punk gigs, Buzzcocks fans are attacked by mobs of NF/British Movement supporters at this show.

Tues 27th   Coventry, New Theatre

Wed 28th   Aylesbury, Friars

Sat 31st
Buzzcocks' 'UK Mini Tour' ends at the Hammersmith Odeon with Ludus and added support from Patrick Fitzgerald. The concert is recorded by Island Mobile.

April
Mon 2nd
With no plans to gig during the month of April, the band's PA system and members of the road crew are out on hire to The Undertones for their first headlining tour of Britain.

Mon 2nd
Radio 1 broadcast tracks from a pre-recorded session by Buzzcocks on the *Dave Lee Travis Show* throughout the week 2nd-4th April. The session is repeated on the *Simon Bates Show* this same week.

Sat 7th
Sounds feature a two page interview with Shelley.

Tues 17th
Pete Shelley's birthday party takes place at Manchester's Russell Club. Apart from the other band members, the party is attended by members of The Gang of Four, Delta 5, The Mekons and many well-known Manchester faces.

Sat 28th
Shelley appears on the front cover of the *NME*, with an accompanying interview inside.

May
Tues 1st
Buzzcocks are rehearsing at T.J's. A three page interview with Diggle appears in *Zig Zag* magazine.

Thurs 10th-Fri 11th
Buzzcocks rehearsing at Central Sound, 91 St. James' Street, in Manchester.

Mon 14th
Buzzcocks, Mekons and Cabaret Voltaire are filmed playing live by Granada TV's Tony Wilson at the Russell Club for a pilot programme. The gig is not advertised and Buzzcocks only play nine numbers. Unfortunately, since Granada TV are experimenting with a new recording technique, serious problems arise resulting in a fault with the synching tones on the video. The programme is never shown.

Sat 19th
Buzzcocks are recording their next single at Eden Studio, 20-24 Beaumont Road, Acton, London. They record a Diggle composition 'Harmony In My Head' and Shelley's 'Something's Gone Wrong Again'.

Sun 20th
Buzzcocks record at Eden Studios for a second day. After a long session in the studio, the band and crew go to see The Undertones at the London Lyceum.

Mon 21st
Buzzcocks are at BBC Maida Vale, Studio 4, recording four tracks for the *John Peel Show* to be broadcast on May 28th. The tracks are 'I Don't Know What To Do With My Life/Mad Mad Judy/Hollow Inside/ESP'. For the first track, Shelley takes the opening guitar riff from a TV kitchen advert.

Sun 27th
Buzzcocks are fourth on the billing at the Loch Lomond Festival held at Cameron Bear Park, Alexandra, Dunbarton in Scotland. Backstage, Shelley talks to Bob Geldof.

June
Sat 2nd
Melody Maker features a report on the Loch Lomond Festival in Scotland.

July
Wed 4th-Thurs 5th
Buzzcocks begin recording demo's for their new, third album *A Different Kind Of Tension* at Arrow Studios, Manchester. The sessions also feature a Garvey composition called 'Running Away From Home'. Although the track is recorded in demo form, it is not included on the album.

Sun 8th-Mon 9th
Buzzcocks move to Eden Studios, London to continue recording their new album. From the first day's sessions comes a future single release entitled 'You Say You Don't Love Me/Raison D'Etre'.

Fri 13th
'Harmony In My Head/Something's Gone Wrong Again' is released as the first single from the album *A Different Kind Of Tension*. Despite the new writing credit, the single still receives positive reviews - *Sounds* say "Diggle's first shot at writing and vocals on an A side is still unmistakably Buzzcocks" whilst *NME* are even more

impressed: "this is one of the most under-rated singles ever." The single continued the Buzzcocks' chart success, giving them their sixth Top 40 hit by reaching No. 32. It is just as well that Diggle's efforts were so well received - by now, a fragile Shelley has retreated into himself even more and the lack of new material is becoming a cause for concern.

Sat 21st
Sounds preview a three day rock festival taking place over the August Bank Holiday in Leigh, hometown of Shelley. Among the bands rumoured to be attending are Buzzcocks, but they do not.

Tues 24th
Buzzcocks are at Air Studios, London recording the re-make of 'Harmony In My Head' for Thursday night's *Top of the Pops* .

Wed 25th
Buzzcocks are at BBC Television Centre recording the actual *Top of the Pops* appearance.

Thurs 26th
Buzzcocks' screened performance is part of *Top of the Pops'* 800th edition.

Fri 27th
Pete Shelley and Steve Diggle attend the *Melody Maker* 'Music Exhibition' at London's Olympia. They mingle with fans and sign autographs.

August
Sat 11th
Buzzcocks have completed the recording for their third album *A Different Kind Of Tension*, which is set for release in September. The album is mixed at Martin Rushent's Genetic Studio in Berkshire, his first project from his own studio.

Wed 15th
A Different Kind Of Tension, is mastered at Portland Studios, London.

Sat 18th
Buzzcocks' planned concert for London's Hyde Park is cancelled

due to lack of record company support and the overwhelming competition provided by The Who playing nearby at Wembley.

Sat 25th
'Spiral Scratch' EP is re-issued. This time it reaches No. 31 in the singles chart. Derry band The Undertones invite Buzzcocks to appear at a free outdoor punk festival in their hometown with The Clash headlining. Buzzcocks are forced to decline owing to financial strain.

Thurs 30th
Buzzcocks make their debut in the USA with a concert at Boston's Paradise club. The band are later interviewed live on WERS-FM.

Fri 31st   New York, Club 57.

September
Sat 1st
Second night at New York, Club 57. During the gig, which is being broadcast live by WPIX FM, a section of the audience mob the band onstage. The band themselves tear down a banner, and only narrowly escape the pursuing bouncers. WPIX-FM also broadcast an interview with Buzzcocks.

Sun 2nd   Long Island, My Father's Place

Tues 4th   Washington D.C., 9:30 Club. Diggle smashes the neck of his 1954 Gibson Les Paul guitar, (serial number 225). The guitar cost him £895.

Wed 5th
Buzzcocks' debut release in the USA, 'Everybody's Happy Nowadays' is issued on the International Record Syndicate Label. United Artists have licenced their records to the label who in turn have a distribution deal with A&M Records.

Buzzcocks and crew fly to Toronto, Canada

Fri 7th   Toronto, Music Hall. The band are interviewed before the concert by the local TV station and a segment of the gig is filmed.

Sat 8th
Buzzcocks and crew fly from Toronto, Canada to Chicago, since tonight's concert in Detroit is been cancelled.

Sun 9th   Chicago, Mother's. During the afternoon, Buzzcocks are interviewed by WZRD Radio and make a personal appearance at a local record store called Waxtrax. The evening's concert is broadcast live by WZRD-FM.

Mon 10th   Minneapolis, Long Hall.
          Members of The Clash attend the concert.

Tues 11th   San Francisco, Greary Temple

Wed 12th   Santa Monica, Civic Centre

Fri 14th
A Different Kind Of Tension, the band's third album is released in the UK. The photograph used on the twelve track album sleeve is taken on Westminster Bridge, and is placed on a yellow and triangular montage. The record labels themselves carry the titles 'Thorn Beneath The Rose' and 'The Rose On The Chocolate Box', taken from a Jon Savage review of *Love Bites* (*Sounds* 23rd September 1978) - the title of this same review is 'Another Kind Of Tension'.

By this release, Shelley appeared to be on the verge of a nervous breakdown, and some saw the LP as a post mortem of his emotions. The songs were perhaps a final farewell to Shelley the romantic, which, unfortunately for many, was the core appeal of Buzzcocks.

Despite the record reaching only No. 26, their worst album placing thus far, the record receivs better reviews in many senses than both its predecessors. *NME* say "Musically, the album has a consistency that wasn't achieved by either *Another Music* or the messy *Love Bites*. This album shows Pete Shelley to be so much more than a craftsman." *Sounds* is equally positive, saying "It is the best Buzzcocks album because it is honest and self-critical, all to real - real feelings, real standards, and real tears." Only *Melody Maker* holds major reservations: "what do you get when a band as potentially great as Buzzcocks makes an album that veers from the brilliant and inspired to the downright dreadful?"

Sat 15th　　　New York, Diplomat Hotel. Buzzcocks appear on the front cover of *Melody Maker*, photographed in New York's China Town. Inside is a two-page spread on their highly successful American tour.

Sun 16th
Return to London..

Wed 19th
American Buzzcocks fan Joan McNulty publishes the first of the US fan newsletter 'Harmony In My Head'. Over the four years that it exists, the newsletter runs for 19 issues, folding in November 1983 with a mailing list of over 5,000 members worldwide.

Sat 22nd
Record Mirror review Buzzcocks' third album *A Different Kind Of Tension*.

Tues 25th
Buzzcocks' debut album release in the US, entitled *Singles Going Steady*, is issued on the IRS Label. The photograph used for the sleeve was taken at Olympic, in Studio 2, on the same day as the shoot for their debut album *Another Music In A Different Kitchen*, and is placed on black rectangular artwork.

'You Say You Don't Love Me' is released.

Sat 29th
Record Mirror cover Buzzcocks' first tour of the US with an article titled "Buzzcocks Over America!", in which Diggle describes their concert at New York's Club 57 thus: "They were screaming and shouting over the top, just like we were The Beatles!"

Sun 30th
Buzzcocks perform a complete live rehearsal with full sound and lights at Middleton Civic Hall in preparation for their extensive forthcoming tour of the UK.

Mon 31st
Buzzcocks rehearse for a second day at Middleton Civic Hall.

Buzzcocks are banned by Wigan!

THE BUZZCOCKS, who were forced to delay the opening of their British tour when they sacked bassist Garth at short notice, have run into problems with one of their venues — even before the revised opening date of the tour next Tuesday (1). They have been banned from playing Wigan Casino on November 17, following the intervention of the local police.

And the venue has been forced to cancel its Thursday punk night series, because the police will not allow them to hold punk shows of any description. It's ironic that earlier this year the Wigan Council launched a massive publicity campaign to attract visitors to the town!

Buzzcocks on the way to their first tour of Europe, supporting Blondie

Shelley, Garvey and Diggle, Loch Lomond Festival, 27/5/79

With Mike Joyce at Reading, 25/8/90

With Frank Sidebottom, Heaton Park Festival, 3/8/91

During sessions for *Trade Test Transmissions*, 3/93

Buzzcocks, 1993

Pete Shelley, Connor Hall, 13/5/93

Pete Shelley, soundcheck, The Garage, Glasgow, 30/4/94

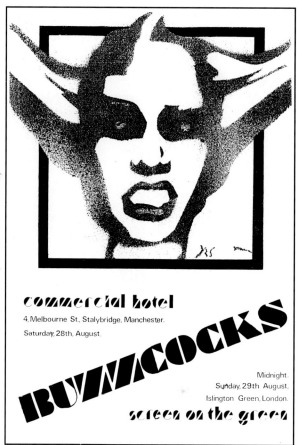

Buzzcocks artwork: Commercial Hotel 1976; first use of official logo by Malcolm Garrett, 1977; Entertaining Friends Tour, 1978;

Don't look over your shoulder, but the Sex Pistols are coming

Sex Pistols

MARQUEE

"HURRY UP, they're having an orgy on stage," said the bloke on the door as he tore the tickets up.

I waded to the front and staightway sighted a chair arcing gracefully through the air, skidding across the stage and thudding contentedly into the PA system, to the obvious nonchalance of the bass drums and guitar.

Well I didn't think they sounded *that* bad on first earful — then I saw it was the singer wh'd done the throwing.

He was stalking round the front rows, apparently scuffing over the litter on the floor between baring his teeth at the audience and stopping to chat to members of the group's retinue. He's called Johnny Rotten and the monicker fits.

Sex Pistols? Seems I'd missed the cavortings with the two scantily clad (plastic thigh boots and bodices) pieces dancing up front. In fact, I only caught the last few numbers; enough, as it happens, to get the idea. Which is . . . a quarter of spiky teenage misfits from the wrong end of various London roads, playing 60's styled white punk rock as unself-consciously as it's possible to play it these days i.e. self-consciously.

Punks? Springsteen Bruce and the rest of 'em would get shredded if they went up against these boys. They've played less than a dozen gigs as yet, have a small but fanatic following, and don't get asked back. Next month they play the Institute of Contemporary Arts if that's a clue.

I'm told the Pistols repertoire includes lesser known Dave Berry and Small Faces numbers (check out early Kinks' B sides leads), besides an Iggy and the Stooges item and several self-penned numbers like the moronic "I'm Pretty Vacant', a meandering power-chord job that produced the chair-throwing incident.

No-one asked for an encore but they did one anyway: "We're going to play 'Substitute'."

"You can't play," heckled an irate French punter.

"So what?" countered the bassman, jutting his chin in the direction of the bewildered Frog.

That's how it is with the Pistols — a musical experience with the emphasis on Experience.

"Actually, we're not into music," one of the Pistols confided afterwards.

Wot then?

"We're into chaos."

Neil Spencer

Pistols' Johnny Rotten: it fits.

Secret Public logo

(Top) The review that started it all, and (Bottom) Shelley in gloomy mood just before the split, in the fan club newsletter

October
Tues 2nd
Buzzcocks' 'Tension Tour' opens at Liverpool, Mountford Hall with Joy Division supporting. The shows on these dates are sub-standard, the band look tired and make little effort to communicate with their audience. This opening night is reviewed by *Melody Maker* as "depressing, so disappointing." The apparent slide of the band towards oblivion is accentuated by the sheer brilliance of the support band.

Wed 3rd   Leeds, University.

Thurs 4th   Newcastle, City Hall.
Sounds review this gig as "same old rubbish in a different theatre."

Fri 5th   Glasgow, Apollo. After the concert, an initially quiet drink in the bar of the Central Hotel soon becomes a night of outrageous 'dare' games between Buzzcocks and Joy Division, resulting in the police being called and Boon receiving a massive bill for the drinks and damage.

A lengthy three-page feature with photographs appears in the *NME*, mirrored by a similar two-page interview with Diggle in *Sounds*.

Sun 7th   Aberdeen, Capitol. The management at Capitol threaten to call the police if the audience do not move back from the stage. Diggle and Maher end the set by attacking their equipment. Later, the band are informed that they will never play the venue again.

Mon 8th   Dundee, Caird Hall. Richard Boon throws a party to celebrate the end of the first leg of the tour.

Wed 10th   Belfast, Ulster Hall (cancelled).

Thurs 11th   Portrush, Kelly's (cancelled).

Sat 13th   Cork, City Hall (cancelled).

Thurs 18th   Bangor University. In the afternoon, crew member Keith Wilde walks out on the tour. Franny Taylor is left to get the PA together just as the doors are opening. There are no soundchecks, but the band perform brilliantly regardless.

Sat 20th   Loughborough, University.

Sun 21st   Sheffield, Top Rank.

Mon 22nd   Derby, Assembly Rooms.

Tues 23rd   Blackburn, King George's Hall.

Wed 24th   Birmingham, Odeon.

Thurs 25th   Bradford, St. George's Hall. The band are interviewed by Radio Leeds at the Norfolk Gardens Hotel where they are staying, before the 4.00pm soundcheck.

Sat 27th   Manchester, Apollo.

Sun 28th   Manchester, Apollo.

Mon 29th   Leicester, De Montford Hall.

Tues 30th   Oxford, New Theatre.

November
Thurs 1st   Guildford, Civic Hall.

Fri 2nd   Bournemouth, Winter Gardens.

Sat 3rd   Cardiff, Sophia Gardens (cancelled)

Sun 4th   Bristol, Colston Hall.

Mon 5th   Hemel Hempstead, Pavilion.

Wed 7th   West Runton, Pavilion.

Fri 9th   London, Rainbow Theatre. Surprisingly, tonight's show is superb, the exception in a series of poor performances.

Sat 10th
Buzzcocks' 'Tension Tour' ends with a second night at the Rainbow Theatre. Support band Joy Division end the tour in high jinks - during the gig they dump fishing maggots on the sound and lighting desks, spray the crew with shaving foam, put live mice through the windows of the tour vans and bombard the crew with eggs before finally being chased off by a passing police car. Both nights at the Rainbow Theatre are recorded.

Sun 25th
The band and crew, without Shelley, fly to New York. Shelley flies over on Concorde and they all meet up at New York's, Gramercy Park Hotel. On these dates, crowds are down and performances are inferior to the UK dates of the previous weeks.

Mon 26th   Boston, The Paradise.

Tues 27th
The band and crew visit the famous Max's club in Kansas City.

Wed 28th   Emerald City, Cherry Hills, Philadelphia.

Thurs 29th   Asbury Park, The Fast Lane, Jersey. While having a drink in a bar before the gig, the bartender informs Maher that he is sitting in Bruce Springsteen's favourite seat.

Fri 30th   Buzzcocks go to see Wreckless Eric at Hurrah's Club

December
Sat 1st   New York, Palladium Theatre, with support The Cramps. The concert is recorded by WNEW FM New York and is broadcast the following week, December 6th. Unfortunately for Buzzcocks, the music media deride the depressing half-filled show.

Mon 3rd   Chicago, Park West, again with supporting group The Cramps.

Wed 5th   Kansas City, Lawrence Opera House, same support.

Thurs 6th   Oklahoma City, Norman Boomer Theatre, supported this time by Ultravox. Meanwhile, WNEW FM broadcast the concert from New York's Palladium Theatre.

Fri 7th   Dallas, Western Place (cancelled due to poor ticket sales). Instead, Buzzcocks travel on to Houston.

Sat 8th   Houston, Palace Theatre. Garvey gets punched in the mouth by one of two off-duty policemen, as he attempts to get fans backstage.

After the gig, a group of girls invite the band and crew to a party being thrown by the legendary Mingle Brothers. These are a duo who achieved legendary status in Houston, Texas for their infamous party-throwing and celebrity mingling. Visiting bands were invited to their parties, which were always overflowing with alcohol, girls and other excess. Friends of theirs were called Minglers.

Sun 9th
Buzzcocks have three days rest and go clubbing and sight-seeing in Los Angeles, staying at the Holiday Inn.

Mon 10th   New Orleans, Tentative (cancelled). The band and crew stay on in Los Angeles.

Wed 12th   Los Angeles, Stardust Club with support The Cramps.

Fri 14th   Santa Cruz, Catalyst

Sat 15th   San Francisco, Greary Temple. The concert is broadcast live by KALX-FM San Francisco radio.

Sun 16th
Band and crew are due to fly back to England today, but the airline refuses to confirm Boon's American Express card until it can be verified with their London office, which puts their return trip home back a day. The band are forced to check into the Airport Hilton. Shelley, ravaged by the exhaustive schedules, band difficulties and his increasingly weak mental and physical state, announces that they will take at least one year off from touring. Privately, crew member Franny Taylor believes this is the end of the Buzzcocks.

| Mon 17th | Buzzcocks leave New York for the UK. |

| Tues 18th | Washington, Showbox (cancelled) |

1980

January
Thurs 17th
At Deville's Club, Manchester, Maher watches The Things, meets vocalist Tim Lyon and tells him he thinks they are the best local band.

Sun 20th
Maher writes an editorial letter for the *Secret Public* fan club newsletter (No.4)

Tues 29th
Maher and Boon attend a second gig by The Things, this time at Salford Technical College. Maher asks the band if they would like to record a single for his own newly-formed Imperial Records label, but since they are looking for a better drummer, they only agree to the deal if Maher joins the band himself. The arrangement is agreed with a handshake.

Thurs 31st
Tim Chacksfield leaves his job as A&R with United Artists. He is replaced by Graham Fletcher.

February
Fri 8th
Buzzcocks are in the studio recording demo's for four new Steve Diggle compositions.

March
Fri 14th
United Artists lose their independence after being taken over by EMI Records, thus becoming Liberty/United.

| Wed 19th | Shelley writes an editorial for *Secret Public* (No.5) |

| Sat 22nd | Shelley leaves for a holiday in Italy. |

April
Tues 1st
Shelley writes 'I Look Alone' in the courtyard of the Hotel Tramontano, Sorrento between 10.00am and 12.00 mid-day. It is one of only three songs that he writes all year.

Fri 18th-Mon 21st
Rehearsing and recording begins for new material towards their next project, 'Parts 1-3', at Pluto Studios, Cheshire, with Martin Hannett.

Mon 21st
Maher celebrates the end of his teens with a party at the studio, on this last day of the new sessions. Later, Diggle joins Sham 69 onstage at Manchester's Apollo Theatre for two numbers, 'If the Kids Are United', and 'Borstal Breakout'.

Fri 25th
Maher and bassist Joe Brehony make their debut with The Things at The Lincoln Inn in Liverpool. Maher's association with The Things lasted for only eleven gigs, and never encroached upon his obligations with Buzzcocks, who themselves never saw his involvement with another band as an issue.

May
Sun 11th
Buzzcocks continue working on new material, this time at Advision Studios in London with Martin Hannett. Backing tracks are completed for their next three singles.

Mon 12th-Wed 14th
Recording at Advision Studios, London.

Thurs 15th
Buzzcocks move to Townhouse Studios to start mixing. They put finishing touches to 'Are Everything' before moving north to Strawberry Studios in Stockport where they complete recordings for 'Why She's A Girl From The Chainstore/Strange Thing/Airwaves Dream'. Buzzcocks were now hitting the depths of their excess. In *Product*, Shelley talks with openness about the band's drug use when he says "We started doing Parts 1-3, that was rock 'n' roll city, where the coke came and the heroin and the acid and the dope. I got very

withdrawn; I'd painted myself into a corner as far as the songs went. There were times when we wouldn't start work until 2 o'clock because we were waiting for the drugs." Shelley also said of the drug use that "it made it easier to work, but nothing was getting done." Apparently, 'Are Everything' was done whilst both he and producer Martin Hannett were tripping. During these sessions, Garvey vanished, and was later said to have gone horse racing, which clearly did little to help the band. Later, Garvey said of this "I wasn't happy with the way things were going. Shelley was out of his mind on drugs and the songs were not good. I guess I knew the end was near."

Sat 17th
Record Mirror report that Buzzcocks are "well over half-way towards completing a fourth album". The band have been using brass and strings in their studio sessions.

Sun 18th
Joy Division's Ian Curtis is found dead in his Manchester home, on the eve of his band's American tour. Suicide is suspected.

Wed 21st
The Things, featuring Maher on drums, play The Beach Club in Manchester.

Thurs 22nd
The Radio 1 Roadshow joins a Buzzcocks performance at Manchester Polytechnic in order to broadcast part of the set live. This one-off concert in their hometown is their first gig in five months, peculiar for such a prolific touring group. Shelley dedicates 'Strange Thing' to the memory of Ian Curtis, a song about depression that Shelley recorded the vocals for whilst on anti-depressants himself. They preview some new material, but there is an air of doom around the show, which some rumours suggest will be their last ever. It is well known that Shelley's writing drought is continuing. The same week, Shelley tells *Zig Zag* magazine that "Buzzcocks' popularity has not grown since 1978."

Sat 24th
The Things' support The Damned at Manchester's Russell Club.

Mon 26th
The Things play Manchester's Band on the Wall.

Wed 28th
Maher plays with two bands at Manchester's Portland Bars, namely The Things and The Renegades. Maher only played a handful of gigs with The Renegades, and never recorded with them.

June
Sat 7th
Record Mirror review Buzzcocks' concert at Manchester Polytechnic. (from May 22nd)

Wed 11th
The Things, (with Maher), are at Cargo Studios in Rochdale, recording their debut single 'Pieces Of You/Lost Love', for release on Imperial Records.

July
Tues 1st
The Things record four songs for a Picadilly Radio session, including 'Pleasures Of The Mind/Time And Time Again/Pieces Of You/If You're There On Time'.

Sat 12th
Picadilly Radio broadcast the debut session by The Things from the previous night.

August
Sat 16th
Although Buzzcocks have been inactive for almost a year, the solo projects of various members have been developing. Steve Garvey has continued both gigging and recording with The Teardrops, whilst John Maher has been performing not only with the aforementioned Renegades and Things, but also with Pauline Murray & The Invisible Girls (as lead singer with Penetration, Murray had covered Buzzcocks' 'Nostalgia' for that band's *Moving Targets* album). Shelley himself had embarked on a solo album, whilst Diggle had enlisted the help of Garvey and Maher to record a solo EP of his, due for release in February. The solo activity of Buzzcocks members becomes very complex from hereon, and the

discography best explains the various band permutations and line ups of all of the many projects.

A review of Shelley's solo release *Sky Yen* (released 24/4/80) appears in *Sounds*, opening with the words "Poor, Pete Shelley!" Recorded largely on an oscillator, the record consists of random electronic noise, very much influenced by Eno, and is at times unlistenable.

Tues 19-Thurs 21st
Diggle, Garvey and Maher are at Cargo Studio in Rochdale recording the solo EP he has written, entitled 'Fifty Years Of Comparative Wealth', containing three Diggle compositions. This solo recording is booked and paid for by New Hormones.

Sat 23rd
NME report that Buzzcocks are set to release the first in a series of singles: 'Part 1' consists of two songs, 'Are Everything' and 'Why She's A Girl From The Chainstore'. The sleeve is designed to emphasise the fact that the record has no A or B side. Unfortunately, the commercial success of this single (and indeed the Parts 2 and 3) is very reserved. This first part reaches only No. 61, their poorest position in the chart ever. (apart from 'Spiral Scratch' which did not chart and 'Orgasm Addict' which received a crippling air time ban).

Tues 26th
'Are Everything/Why She's A Girl From The Chainstore' is released. 'Are Everything' features Geoff Richardson from Caravan on viola and George Born from Henry Cow And The Feminist Improvisation Group, on cello.

Sat 30th
To promote 'Are Everything', Buzzcocks make a live appearance on Granada TV's Saturday morning children's programme *Fun Factory*. The band mime on set while children surround Maher's drum kit. The TV crew dress in animal suits for what is the last show of the series.

To promote 'Why She's A Girl From The Chainstore', the band film a video in the Manchester branch of Lewis' department store, with Linder playing the part of a robotic check-out girl. The video also contains a party scene featuring Shelley's mother and late father, shot at his parents' home in Leigh. Later, despite Shelley's former announcements to the contrary, the press report that Buzzcocks have decided to tour after all.

September
Mon 1st
Garvey's partly owned race horse Regent's Boy dies. He was three years old.

Fri 5th
Buzzcocks are featured in the *Manchester Evening News* with the headline "Back Buzz The Cocks!"

Sat 27th
Buzzcocks announce their plans for the remainder of the year in the music press, the main focus of which is their 'Tour By Instalments' - 'Phase 1, 2 and 3', a series of dates intended to keep themselves fresh. In fact, the tours fell apart after Phase 1.

October
Fri 3rd
'Pieces Of You/Lost Love', the debut single by The Things is released on Imperial Records, and proves to be the label's first and last release.

Tues 7th
Buzzcocks are at Genetic Studios with Martin Rushent mixing 'Running Free/What Do You Know?/I Look Alone' (October 7th-12th).

Fri 10th
The Things play Manchester's Russell Club with Maher on drums.

Sat 11th
A review of Pauline Murray & The Invisible Girls debut album is featured in *Sounds*. The album's drummer is also John Maher.

Sun 12th
Buzzcocks complete work at Genetic Studios.

Mon 13th
'Part 2' - 'Strange Thing/Airwaves Dream' is released. Again the release is poorly received, this time failing to chart altogether. In an attempt to find a long lost friend, Shelley puts a message on the sleeve of the single that reads "Where is Paul King?" Two days after the release, Paul King rings Shelley from Scotland.

Fri 24th
Buzzcocks are due to receive their annual advance from Virgin Publishers, but this is withheld as the band have not yet released a fourth album.

Wed 29th
'Phase 1' of Buzzcocks' 'Tour By Instalments' opens at Sheffield's City Hall. Support on the tour is The Things which features Maher on drums. Since the tour only amounted to eight gigs and with the Buzzcocks set lasting no more than 45 minutes, Maher was easily able to accommodate both groups. Ironically, this short tour was originally designed as one last ditch attempt to pull together a disintegrating band - unfortunately, this 'comeback' gig was very poorly attended, with the half-empty hall containing only just over 400 people. *Record Mirror* called it "the big come-back tour to which nobody came." Onstage, the band were clearly struggling, with large silent gaps between songs and Shelley standing motionless centre stage.

Thurs 30th   Birmingham, Odeon

Fri 31st
Garvey rehearses with two friends, Dave Price and Dave Rowbotham for an as yet unnamed new band. Rowbotham later played with The Frantic Elevators (who later became Simply Red). With so much solo activity, the future of Buzzcocks looked bleak. Shelley himself was now paranoid and desperately unhappy, and appeared to have dried up creatively. Buzzcocks as a unit were struggling under the pressure of living out of each other's pockets constantly and therefore the appeal of side projects grew. Of these new developments, Garvey was perhaps the most pragmatic, and in his opinion it was now already over: "Buzzcocks died of natural causes, it should have happened a year ago."

November

Sat 1st   Woolwich, Thames Polytechnic Students Union.

Sun 2nd   London, Lyceum with added support from the Au Pairs and Orange Juice. After the encore, Diggle kicks his amplifier to the ground and Maher smashes his drum kit.

Mon 3rd
Buzzcocks travel from London to Manchester, driven by tour manager Pete Monks. Shelley sits in the back seat with Diggle and Garvey. In the front is the band's personal minder 'Sarge'. Maher has already left London with his girlfriend at 7.00am. The band are interviewed upon their arrival in Manchester by the *NME*.

Despite all these developments, after tonight's show at Manchester's Apollo Theatre, the band hold a party for relatives and friends in the dressing room, and amongst those present are both Shelley's parents.

Thurs 4th
Shelley and vocalist with The Things, Tim Lyons review the latest record releases on Picadilly Radio's *Transmission* programme, hosted by Mark Radcliffe.

Wed 5th   Blackburn, King George's Hall

Thurs 6th   Glasgow, Apollo Theatre

Sat 8th
Record Mirror review Buzzcocks' concert at Sheffield City Hall with the headline "Will They Survive?"

Sun 16th
Buzzcocks fly from Manchester Airport to Boston, via London Heathrow.

Mon 17th
Joan McNulty, who still runs the Buzzcocks information sheet 'Harmony In My Head' in the USA, meets the band on their arrival in America and drives them to various TV and radio stations during their stay. Their first interview is a live transmission at 12 noon on

Radio WMBR's *Late Risers Club*. The band then return to The Bradford Hotel where they are interviewed at 3.00pm by Boston Rock newspaper. At 9.30pm the band make a live appearance on Radio WERS followed by a 12midnight live appearance on Radio WBCN's *Oedipus Show*. This first day is typical of the intense media attention once more afforded to Buzzcocks during their stay in America.

Tues 18th   Amherst, Rusty Nail

Wed 19th   Willimantic, Shaboo

Fri 21st   Long Island, My Father's Place. Buzzcocks are
                interviewed on WVHC-FM-Long Island, New.

Sat 22nd
After a 5.00pm soundcheck the band are interviewed by *New Sound Magazine*. At 7.00pm they are taken by limo to a rock and roll flea market. Tonight, they play New Jersey, Emerald City. After the show, they are interviewed by Radio WMMR, *Rock Ages* and *Terminal* magazines.

Sun 23rd   New York, The Ritz

Mon 24th   Rhode Island, Brown University, Alumni Hall

'What Do You Know?/Running Free' (Part 3) is released in the UK. In America, 'Parts 1-3' were released on a 12". Like the two preceding parts, this release fairs very poorly, charting at No.120 but soon dropping to No. 135, then out of the chart altogether.

Tues 25th   Boston, Bradford Hotel Ballroom.
                The concert is filmed by Boston's Channel 68 TV.

Wed 26th   Buzzcocks are guest DJ's on WBCN Radio from noon
to 1.00pm. At 7.15pm, they fly out from Boston back to Heathrow.

Thurs 27th
Buzzcocks arrive at London Heathrow and take a BA Shuttle to Manchester Airport.

Fri 28th
Manchester Evening News features a full page article on Buzzcocks.

December
Sat 13th
'Phase 2' of 'Tour By Instalments' is due to open at Bolton's Sports Centre, but the concert is cancelled and instead rescheduled for December 20th.

Sun 14th   Derby, Romeo and Juliets (cancelled). A management statement was released which stated the cause of cancellation as "recording commitments", but Shelley has since said this decision was made at a meeting that was deliberately conducted in his absence. The band are forced to abandon 'Phase 2' of their 'Tour By Instalments'. The rescheduled dates never happen.

Mon 15th   Liverpool, Royal Court (cancelled).

Tues 16th   Leeds, Polytechnic (cancelled).

Wed 17th   Middlesborough, Town Hall.

Sat 20th
Buzzcocks manage to play the rescehduled Bolton's Sports Centre gig. The concert is advertised in the *Secret Public* newsletter as a "fan-club party". The audience are given party hats, Shelley plays 'Auld Lang Syne', and pieces of gold tinsel hang around Maher's drum kit, adding to the Christmas atmosphere. Ex-Pistols Steve Jones and Paul Cook attend the concert.
Plans for a tour of the east coast of America in the New Year are abandoned.

1981

January
Mon 5th   The Things play Manchester's Band on the Wall.

Wed 21st
Buzzcocks' crew leave early for Friday's Rockpalast concert, which is being filmed for German TV. The band leave Hull on a later sailing, arriving in Rotterdam at 8.00am the following morning.

Thurs 22nd
The band drive the 250 miles from Rotterdam to Hamburg where they meet up with the crew.

Fri 23rd
Buzzcocks and crew arrive at the Markethalle venue at noon for a soundcheck. After television checks all afternoon, the doors finally open at 7.30pm. Buzzcocks, with no support, are onstage at 8.30pm playing for one hour. This is the last concert they ever play together as a band.

Mon 26th
Shelley writes notes for the sleeve of a compilation release by Rough Trade/*NME* of a cassette containing what becomes the last recording made by the band, 'I Look Alone'. This track was originally earmarked by Buzzcocks as 'Part 4' but was later offered to the *NME* with a very bizarre mix of 'Strange Thing'(which was rejected, as *NME* only wanted unreleased material). The cassette, entitled 'C-81' is available to readers of the *NME* who collect two coupons from February issues of the music paper and send them with £1.50 to Rough Trade.

Buzzcocks assemble at Pluto Studios to record a fourth album. Bassist Steve Garvey recalls "It was obvious things were not good. With United Artists being taken over by EMI Records, our new A&R Representative had very little interest in us. The money was very tight." A good example of the negligence of the Buzzcocks once the take-over had taken place is the appalling treatment of the master of their excellent *A Different Kind Of Tension* album. When Virgin in France wanted to release the album over there, they asked for a master, but comically EMI did not know where it was. The farce was only resolved when Richard Boon had to go to the EMI offices in Manchester Square in London himself, and physically rummage round their dusty cupboards until he found what was needed.

Producer Martin Rushent had just returned from eight weeks in America, and he too could see that things were deteriorating: "The band had just returned from the States and wanted to stay in Manchester so they went to Pluto Studios for the forth album. I wanted to be in London. Pete was very depressed, there were arguments. Nothing felt right." Richard Boon was also there: "When we got to Pluto Studios, there was not even a bass amplifier. EMI had taken over and suddenly Buzzcocks were this thing in a filing cabinet in some office that no-one wanted to deal with."

To add to the band's misery, the financial state of their affairs was dire - Shelley has since said that this was perhaps the key reason for the eventual split. The tours in America had ravaged their cash situation, and the lack of supposed tour support from appropriate parties meant the band were as good as destitute, financially crippled. This added to the already tense atmosphere.

Tues 27th
Diggle has recorded five numbers on a Porta-studio at home. They are 'Can You Dig It/Drift Away/Dancing At Dawn/By My Side/Don't Come Back'.

Wed 28th
Buzzcocks record a Garvey composition called 'No Friend Of Mine' at Pluto Studios. The track features Garvey on rhythm guitar and vocals.

February
Mon 9th
Martin Rushent suspends the recording of a Buzzcocks' fourth album at Pluto as EMI refuse to come up with the advance to cover recording costs, exacerbating Buzzcocks already desperate financial state. Rushent sees at first hand the disillusionment now in Shelley: "Pete wasn't happy, and when I asked him what was wrong, all he could say was "I want to leave the band, I want to do something different." He had a lot of songs the rest of the band didn't think were suitable."

Wed 11th
While the deadlock with EMI is being discussed, Shelley goes to Martin Rushent's own studio to start work on more album material, but what are thought to be Buzzcocks demo's become the basis of Shelley's solo career. Much of the work was written in 1973 during Shelley's Jets Of Air days.

Steve Garvey felt that Martin Rushent's intervention did not help the band, who were rapidly falling apart: "It was unlike Pete, but he had very few songs, just a few riffs. Rushent took him to his little country studio and from there decided that he didn't need the band." However, Boon defends Martin Rushent's actions: "Martin walked into this situation and in all fairness took Peter aside and said "You shouldn't be dealing with this!" and took him to his own studio. I went down there and Pete told me "Go back to Manchester and dismantle everything." The first thing I did was phone Chris Bohn at the *NME* newsdesk and tell him this was the most exciting thing Buzzcocks had ever done, and bless him, he printed it."

Fri 13th
On the first day of recording, Shelley and Rushent record a version of 'Maxine' which is later released with 'I Don't Know What It Is'. The session continues the following day with Shelley using a Yahama 12-string acoustic guitar borrowed from Pete Monks.

Sat 14th
Shelley records 'Homosapien/Pusher Man/I Generate A Feeling'. Both Shelley and Rushent are so pleased with the results that the temptation for Shelley to leave the band accelerates. Shelley is excited by the freedom away from the enormous restrictions on his immense creativity which the Buzzcocks had become. Now he has no touring schedules to worry about, no band politics, no power struggles, just his music. The ideas which he had found increasingly hard to put across to the band were now there to be tried. Curiously, apart from 'Qu'est-Ce Que C'est Que Ca' (which he writes during the sessions), and 'I Generate A Feeling' (written earlier this year), the new project consists entirely of songs written in 1974. On the strength of these demo's, Shelley signs to Rushent's Genetic Records, with Rushent saying "Buzzcocks felt trapped in the three minute pop format. They were very good at it, but Shelley got bored." The liberation of these sessions confirm for Shelley what he had suspected for some time - that Buzzcocks had long since achieved what they had set out to do.

Sat 28th
Steve Diggle releases his solo EP entitled 'Fifty Years Of Comparative Wealth' on Liberty, recorded with Maher and Garvey, amid increasing speculation that Buzzcocks have finally split.

March
Mon 2nd
Howard Devoto gets a call from Richard Boon telling him that Buzzcocks are on the verge of a split. Devoto himself is in the process of bringing his own band Magazine to an end.

Meanwhile, using a porta-studio that he bought several months ago, Shelley and Francis Cookson start work on a second Tiller Boys album. Although the album is recorded, mixed and transferred to 1/4" tape, and even given the title *Strange Men In Sheds With Spanners*, it is never released.

Wed 4th
Shelley's solicitor sends a letter to Buzzcocks' manager Boon informing him that his client "has reluctantly come to the conclusion that he cannot continue with the band" and requests that Boon speaks to the remaining members of the band before a formal notice is sent to them all.

Fri 6th
Steve Garvey, Steve Diggle and John Maher receive letters from Shelley's solicitor announcing that he has left the band.

Sat 28th
New Musical Express report that Buzzcocks have split with the headline "Ever Fallen Out With Someone....?"

April
Fri 3rd
A statement from EMI records claims the Buzzcocks are "collectively or individually" still signed to that label. Until the dispute is settled, all work has ground to a halt while solicitors battle it out. Soon after, Steve Diggle told the *NME* "To start with it was great, we were always doing something, touring, recording, photo sessions, interviews and rehearsing. Then it all started to fall to pieces. A hell of a lot of money got wasted, some of the artistic and business decisions were ridiculous. We could have done so much better than we did."

Steve Garvey has his own ideas about the split: "After five years of touring we were broke, we had been badly managed. I had come up with a few great riffs in rehearsal and soundcheck but Pete and Steve Diggle never made much of an effort to come up with the lyrics or melody."

In an exclusive interview, also with the *NME*, Pete Shelley comments "I don't think I'll ever be a Buzzcock again."

1982-1988

In the aftermath of punk, music once again fractured into a thousand different shards. Soul and funk were making a resurgence, partly because of the new interest in vintage Stax and Tamla Motown following the Mod revival, but chiefly because black music had been ignored throughout the new wave years, and was bristling to make a comeback. The gloomy 'new existentialist' movement, led by Echo And The Bunnymen, New Order, the Cure and Theatre Of Hate, was also blooming, together with a new breed of pseudo-intellectual music journalism which tried to explain why. In 1981, 'New Pop' emerged, with funky guitars and up-beat brass fills taking the place of traditional white rock instruments, while a fiddle-while-Thatcher-burns-us-all philosophy heralded a return to good ol' fashioned musical escapism. Indeed, an anything-goes atmosphere prevailed — just so long as that anything wasn't punk.

The truth was that, to survive, Buzzcocks would've had to reinvent themselves in some way or other. As it happened, the various members pursued their developing solo interests throughout the decade, all of which displayed the fragmented musical ambitions that had ultimately throttled the very life out of the Buzzcocks.

While Shelley had been desperately eager to cast the Buzzcocks myth aside, Steve Garvey formed his own band Motivation. The line-up consisted of Dave Price on vocals, Dave Rowbotham on guitar, Garvey on bass and Snuff on drums. Initially, the band faired well in the UK, and there was some degree of interest from record companies, but this failed to materialise and eventually led to the departure of Rowbotham and Snuff, leaving Garvey and Price without a deal or band. They regrouped and made some progress, but after a possible record deal with CBS Records fell through, and they sacked their manager, things looked bleak. Early in 1982, Garvey moved to New York where he had hoped to begin work with the band afresh. Unfortunately, a continued lack of record company interest forced the band to finally split up. All that remains of Motivation is an excellent six track demo, recorded at Skyline Studios in New York. Unable to sustain a permanent line up, the session features Garvey on both guitar and bass, complemented by the superb vocals of Dave Price. Motivation's most popular live tracks were 'Excuse Me' and 'Heart Under Cover' the latter of which was even considered for the multi-million-selling Michael Jackson album 'Thriller'. Once the band had split, Garvey went on to work in the docks.

Since September 1980, Steve Diggle had been preparing for the launch of his solo career. The release of his solo EP 'Fifty Years of Comparative Wealth' pre-empted the birth of his new band Flag of Convenience, who played their debut gig at Fagins in Manchester on 14th April 1982. Diggle felt liberated away from the Buzzcocks mould, and the band's material was of sufficient quality to earn a deal with Sire Records shortly after. Unfortunately, Flag of Convenience experienced several line-up changes and as Shelley's successful solo return gathered momentum, the pressure was on to see how Diggle would respond.

Meanwhile, Shelley had become a solo artist in his own right, fascinated by the new technologies that were shaping a lot of other pop music. Buzzcocks as a synth-pop band just wouldn't have worked: one needs only to look at other outfits who took this course - the Angelic Upstarts and 999, for example — to see why. He settled his differences with EMI, leaving him free to sign a solo deal with Island and quickly put the finishing touches to his debut album. Unfortunately, many observers saw the excellent *Homosapien* as an album of left overs from the Buzzcocks era - they could not have been more wrong. The record was in fact virtually all written pre-1976, and as such displayed the heavy Bowie influence on Shelley in those pre-Buzzcocks days. The quality of the debut solo album surprised many, and the dynamic title track was a hit in England, Australia and many parts of Europe despite being banned by the BBC who declared it had 'gay overtones'.

His first solo tour of the UK and America called 'The Man And Machine Tour' opened in Glasgow with a line-up that featured Shelley on guitar and vocals, Steve Garvey on bass, Jim Russell on drums and a backing tape produced by Martin Rushent. A second solo album *XL.1* (which came with its own computer programme) was followed by another major UK tour in the autumn of 1983, a series of dates preceded by a clutch of one-off gigs in London.

Shelley then began a new partnership with Phonogram, and after almost a three year recording silence he released 'Waiting For Love' from the new *Heaven and the Sea* album and toured with a new five-piece band.

With all this solo activity, the chance of Buzzcocks ever reforming was completely out of the question. When asked on the *Old Grey Whistle Test* in 1985 if the rumours of a Buzzcocks comeback were true, Shelley dismissively replied "They say The Beatles are getting back together too." The following year it was even more apparent when at the 'Festival Of The Tenth Summer' in Manchester, a bloated and nostalgic celebration of punk's tenth anniversary, Shelley launched his new three piece band Zip, Steve Diggle performed with F.O.C and Howard Devoto fronted the one-off Adultery which later became Luxuria. Zip in fact played support to Erasure in a massive sell out UK tour in 1988.

Besides, how relevant were Buzzcocks anymore? Music is a fickle monster, and there were genuine fears of a horrid and bloated nostalgic reunion, tainting the glorious memory of the original. As the 80's progressed, however, the importance of Buzzcocks and their immense musical legacy became increasingly apparent. Somehow, as their untimely split receded into the distance, Buzzcocks began to make even more sense. With many indie bands citing a vintage Buzzcocks hit or two among their all-time favourite songs, and just about everyone agreeing that the group had concocted a classic pop-punk formula which was far easier to admire than to emulate, the interest in the band grew. Their 'greatest hits' compilation, *Singles Going Steady*, became a perennial favourite of every self-respecting music fan young and old, and in the mid '80s, it heavily influenced the 'C-86' indie explosion, whose proponents borrowed the group's angular buzz-saw guitars and nonchalant gift for a spot-on melody, and mixed them with Buzzcocks-style romantic pop alienation. Another influence on the late '80s indie scene was Scottish post-punk act Orange Juice, who had expressed their affection for Shelley and Co. by name-dropping 'Spiral Scratch' in their 1983 hit, 'Rip It Up': "You know me, I'm acting dumb-dumb/And the scene is very hum-drum/And my favourite song's entitled 'Boredom'." The links between indie and Buzzcocks were clear for everyone to see. Music journalist David Swift's band even called itself the Razor Cuts (from the lyrics to 'Love You More').

Buzzcocks reforming would never have happened if the various solo projects had been runaway successes. However, by the second half of the decade, Flag of Convenience were still having only a limited impact, and when a French promoter billed the band as 'Buzzcocks F.O.C.', rumours of a reunion quickly spread. Then the Midlands band Fine Young Cannibals recorded their version of 'Ever

Fallen in Love?', (for the Jonathan Demmie film *Something Wild*) which was a Top 10 single, and it was now clear that maybe there was a place for Buzzcocks again after all. In an unusual twist of circumstances, Steve Diggle was reportedly 'kicked out' of Buzzcocks F.O.C. after which Shelley spoke openly of the possibility of a Buzzcocks reunion, something which he had always firmly denied in the past. Shelley's manager then received an offer from American agent Ian Copeland at Frontier Booking International for a re-union US tour. Shortly after, the press were informed - Buzzcocks were back.

1989-1995

When Buzzcocks reformed it was initially the same line up which had split in 1981, and they quickly resumed their close friendship which had initially made the band such a close unit - Shelley said of the reunion and the subsequent ease with which they started playing again: "It was really good, quite easy in fact. We started playing songs and it was just like riding a bike, and afterwards in the pub we just fell about laughing." However, after a UK tour, original drummer John Maher left due to commitments to his drag racing business. The tour tied in with the re-release of the bands entire catalogue in a box set by EMI Records called *Product*. As word spread of their reunion, tour offers came from Britain, Australia and Europe. Maher was replaced by ex-Smiths drummer Mike Joyce, himself a Buzzcocks fan, originally inspired to start playing after hearing Maher's work. Joyce surprisingly added a fresh spark to the band with his powerful drumming.

Despite their eight year absence in which they had little success as solo artists, in 1990 they were invited to play at the Reading Festival alongside many bands over whom they had held enormous influence, such as The Wedding Present and Neds Atomic Dustbin. They were joined by two other punk acts from the seventies, The Fall and Wire.

Using cash that Shelley had received from the success of the Fine Young Cannibals cover of 'Ever Fallen In Love?', Buzzcocks went to Drone Studios in Manchester and recorded demo's of their new material to shop around the various record companies. Surprisingly however, and despite the series of stunning sell-out shows, the new material interested no-one. Frustrated by lack of record company interest they released four of the demos on their own Planet Pacific label as the 'Alive Tonight' EP. The sub-standard release was poorly received, was issued with little publicity and the choice of tracks were a poor reflection on their new work. Some observers whispered that maybe they had made the wrong decision after all.

After a tour of the US in late 1991 the band remained in New York to record a new album at Green Point studios with producer Bill Laswell, but the tour had exhausted them and the recordings showed it - they never surfaced. On the eve of a European and

Japanese tour, Mike Joyce left to join PiL. and Maher returned to fulfil the dates but left again immediately after. They completed a rescheduled tour of Australia with former Icicle Works drummer Steve Gibson. The difficulties establishing a firm line-up continued when Steve Garvey decided at the end of 1992 that he had had enough, citing the impossibility of commuting between New York where he lived with his wife and two children, and London, where the band were now based.

In August 1992, auditions in London recruited bassist Tony Barber and his friend Phil Barker on drums. Both Barber and Barker had played together in Lack Of Knowledge, so their musical unity was strong, and with Barber being a Buzzcocks fanatic, he knew every track meticulously already. The new line-up added a youthful appeal to the band and the ability of Barber and Barker matched the pace of the original rhythm section - fourteen months of solid touring followed and such was the standard of the shows that by the end Buzzcocks had finally regained the respect of the music world. As yet though, they still remained without a record deal.

In 1993 this dilemma was resolved when the new line-up signed a deal with Castle Communications and finally released their fourth album, entitled *Trade Test Transmissions*. Despite all their problems since reforming, the album was a mighty and complete return to Buzzcocks' brilliance, despite the years separating it from their last release. The critics prepared to destroy yet another 'reunion album', but they were amazed - *Melody Maker* described it as "astonishingly fresh, bright and strong" and said "Buzzcocks are a band with an exciting present as well as a glorious past!".

To promote the album a mammoth world tour followed where the band played a mixture of old and new material. Their profile was boosted still further when Nirvana's Kurt Cobain enlisted them as support for his band's European tour in 1994, a highly successful jaunt only terminated by the tragic suicide of Cobain.

On October 17th 1994, Granada TV featured a half hour special on the band called *With...The Buzzcocks*, containing footage from its previous 1978 special *B'dum B'dum* mixed with more recent interviews and video's of both 'Do It' and 'Libertine Angel'. The band's resurgence continued, stabilised by the now-firm line-up, with a European tour in April 1995, this time recording a live album in Paris for release in July.

1989

(Shelley/Diggle/Garvey/Maher)

TELLING FRIENDS TOUR

Nov 7th	Rhode Island, Providence Living Room
8-9th	Boston, The City Club
10th	New York, The Ritz
11th	Philadelphia, Theatre of the Living Arts
12th	New Jersey, Trenton City Gardens
13-14th	Washington, 9:30 Club
16th	Cleveland, Phantasy Theatre
17th	Detroit, St. Andrews Hall
18th	Chicago, Cabaret Metro
19th	Milwaukee, Presidents Room
20th	Minneapolis, First Avenue
24th	San Diego, The Bacchanal
25th	Santa Monica, Civic Auditorium
26th	Ventura CA., Ventura Theatre
27th	San Francisco, I-Beam (2 shows)
28th	Santa Clara CA., One Step Beyond
30th	Reseda CA., Country Club
Dec 1st	Return to UK

UK REUNION TOUR

Dec 7th	Birmingham, Hummingbird
8th	Manchester, Apollo Theatre
9th	Brixton, Academy
11th	Newcastle, Riverside
12th	Glasgow, Barrowlands
13th	Bristol, Studio
14th	Nottingham, Central TV Studio

(John Maher leaves after UK tour and is replaced by ex-Smiths Mike Joyce. Maher wanted to concentrate on his business interests, predominantly the building of customised VW Beetles and drag racing, both of which he had been involved in for some years.)

1990

(Shelley/Diggle/Garvey/Joyce)

AUSTRALASIAN TOUR

Jan 31st	Buzzcocks arrive in Melbourne
Feb 2-3rd	St. Kilda, The Palace
	(Australian TV Countdown film band during
	soundcheck)
5th	Dee Why, The Venue
7th	Revesby, Roundhouse
8th	Canberra, AN. Campus (Interview on *The Noise* TV show)
9th	Coogee, Selina's
	(Interview with 2JJJ-FM before soundcheck)
10th	Coogee, Selina's
13th	Newcastle, Cambridge Tavern
14th	Sylvania, Promises
16-17th	Auckland, Powerstation
20-21st	Sydney, Globe
22nd	Byron Bay, Arts Factory
23rd	Queensland, University
24th	Gold Coast, Playroom

JAPANESE TOUR

Feb 28th	Osaka, Muse Hall
Mar 1st	Tokyo, Club Quattro
2nd	Kawasaki, Club Chitta Kawasaki
3rd	Return to London

Apr 11-12th
The band's renewed profile is reflected by the screening of a Buzzcocks concert filmed at Central Television Studios in Nottingham on 14/12/89. The show is screened on Anglia on 11th April, and on Thames the following night, albeit well after midnight.

May 4-6th
For the first time since reforming, Buzzcocks spend time recording and mixing new material, at Square One Studio in Bury. Unfortunately, no record of the tracks have been kept, and the studio has since closed down.

Aug 8th   Rehearsing at Airplay Enterprises, Denton.
  11th   Sweden, Hultsfred Festival
  22nd   Digbeth, Institute (Mike Joyce's first UK gig)
  25th   Reading Rock Festival
  26th   Belgium, Pukkelpop Festival

Sept 10-12th
Buzzcocks are at Impact Studios, Kent recording more new material.
Amongst the tracks recorded is a 12" dub mix of 'Successful Street'.
It was intended to be released, but the band felt the session did not
go well, so this never happened.

Oct 3rd   Southend, Cliff's Pavillion
  4th   Sheffield, Octagon Theatre
  5th   Leeds, Polytechnic
  7th   Manchester, Academy
  8th   Nottingham, Rock City
  9th   Liverpool, University
  10th   Reading University
  11th   Swansea, Patti Pavilion
             (Personal appearance at Our Price record store)
  13th   Norwich, University of East Anglia

Nov 21-24th
Band are at Drone Studios, Manchester recording album demo's,
produced by Paul Roberts. During the four day session, they record
'Dreaming/Alive Tonight/Never Gonna Give It Up/Wallpaper
World/Successful Street/Who Will Help Me To Forget/Serious
Crime/Why Compromise?'

1991

Jan 20th-26th
Steve Diggle is recording solo tracks at Drone Studios, also with
producer Paul Roberts. Among the tracks he records are 'Wallpaper
World' and 'Wednesday's Flowers', the latter of which he uses on his
'Heated And Rising' EP in 1993.

Feb 13th
Buzzcocks begin recording for a possible album at Drone Studios
with Paul Roberts. The sessions continue during the coming weeks

and after several breaks are completed on April 24th 1991. The band record 'Never Gonna Give It Up/Serious Crime/Dreaming/Last To Know/Run Away From Home/Tranquilliser/Alive Tonight/When Love Turns Around/Isolation/Successful Street/Who Will Help Me To Forget/Why Compromise?/Australia' (a Steve Garvey instrumental). Unhappy with the production however, the group abandon the project.

Apr 30th   Interview on BBC Radio 5

June 10th   Rehearsals at Airplay Enterprises, Denton

June 11th
10.00am-12.30am Central TV film the band performing 'Last To Know' (at Airplay) for the review show *First Night*.
6.00pm BBC Radio Five (Live Session) for the *Hit the North* show, including 'Alive Tonight /Who'll Help Me To Forget/Love You More/Last to Know/Ever Fallen In Love?'. Buzzcocks fan Tony Barber records this radio session - two years later he joins the band.

12th	Rehearsals at Airplay Enterprises, Denton
13th	Newcastle, Riverside
	Central TV transmit Buzzcocks' performance of 'Last To Know' on *First Night*.
14th	Glasgow, Barrowlands
15th	Wolverhampton, Civic Hall
	(Interviewed by BRMB Radio, after soundcheck)
16-17th	London, Town and Country Club
July 11th	Rehearsals in New York
12th	Trenton, City Gardens
13th	Boston, City Club
14th	Providence, R.I. CLub Babyhead
15th	Hoboken, Maxwells
	(After tonight's gig, the band meet REM)
16th	New York, Academy
17th	Washington, D.C., 9.30 Club
19th	Mexico, Tijuana, Iguana's
20th	Los Angeles, Universal Amphitheatre
21st	Santa Clara, One Step Beyond
22nd	San Francisco, I-Beam

Aug 2nd   Coventry, Tic Toc Club
    3rd   Manchester, Heaton Park
This is Mike Joyce's last UK gig - he would soon accept a place in John Lydon's PiL, but completed the forthcoming US dates even so. Meanwhile, BBC Radio broadcast an interview with Shelley and Devoto recorded on the release of the *Times Up* album on Document Records (originally a bootleg) and the re-issue of 'Spiral Scratch' on CD.

FALL 1991 TOUR

Oct 21-22nd   Rehearsals at Greg Rike Productions,
               Altamonte Springs
    23rd   St. Petersburg, FL., Janus Landing
    24th   Ft. Lauderdale, FL., Summers on the Beach
    25th   Jacksonville, FL., Milkbar
    26th   Atlanta, GA., Roxy Theatre
    27th   Chapel Hill, NC., Cat's Cradle
    29th   Norfolk, VA., Boat House
    30th   Charlottesville, VA., Traxx
    31st   Baltimore, MD., Hammerjacks
Nov 1st   New York, The Ritz
    2nd   Philadelphia, The Trocadero
    3rd   Boston, The City Club
    5th   Toronto, Empire
    6th   Cleveland, Ohio, Peabody's Down Under
    7th   Detroit, St. Andrews Hall
    8th   Cincinnati, Ohio, Bogart's
    9th   Chicago, Cabaret Metro
    11th   Bloomington, Ind., Jakes
    12th   St. Louis, Mississippi Nights
               (KPLR TV interview band during soundcheck)
    14th   Columbia, Coliseum
    15th   Omaha, Ranch Bowl
    16th   Madison
    18th   Minneapolis, First Avenue
    20th   Kansas City, The Shadow
    22nd   Denver, 23 Parrish
    23rd   Salt Lake City, Bar and Grill
    25th   Portland, Melody Ballroom
    26th   Vancouver BC., Commodore Ballroom
    27th   Victoria BC., Harpo's

28th	Seattle, Wash., RCKCNDY
30th	San Francisco, I Beam
Dec 1st	St. Louis Obispo, Loco Ranchero
2nd	Palo Alto, The Edge
3rd	Sacramento
4th	Santa Cruz, CA., The Catalyst
5-6th	Los Angeles, The Palace
7th	San Diego, The Bachanal
8th	Plans for the band to fly home are changed, and

instead they fly to New York where they begin recording at Green Point Studio, with Bill Laswell. The sessions continue until 22/12 and are planned for a possible album, but are never released. Tracks recorded are 'Isolation/Never Gonna Give It Up/When Love Turns Around/All Over You/Trash Away/Who Will Help Me To Forget/Run Away From Home/Why Compromise /Alive/ Tonight/Last To Know /Inside/Serious Crime/Tranquilliser/ Dreaming'. Mike Joyce then leaves to join Public Image Ltd.

1992

With Joyce having left virtually overnight, the band's dilemma is solved with a phonecall to Maher, who agrees to fill in the vacant drummer's spot for the forthcoming dates in Europe and Japan only.

(Shelley/Diggle/Garvey/Maher)

Jan 29-30th	Rehearsals at John Henry's (Studio 4), London
31st	London, The Grand
Feb 1st	London, The Grand (Garvey and Maher's last UK gig)
3rd	Cologne, Live Musichall
4th	Munich, Theatrefabrik
5th	Paris, Elysee Montmartre
7th	Amsterdam, Paradiso
8th	Hamburg, Rote Fabrik
9th	Berlin, Neue Welt
10th	Krefeld, Kulturfabrik
11th	Brussels, Ancienne Belgique
14-15th	Tokyo, Club Chitta Kawasaki
17th	Nagoya, Club Quattro
18th	Osaka, Club Quattro

The following six dates are cancelled when John Maher leaves the band after the Japanese dates:

21st	Dee Why, The Venue
22nd	Sydney, Selina's
25th	Perth, Berlin Club
26th	Adelaide, The Old Lion Hotel
27th	Melbourne, The Palace
28th	Brisbane, Metropolis

With Steve Gibson of The Icicle Works as stand-in drummer for the following Australian tour only:

(Shelley/Diggle/Garvey/Gibson)

Apr 21st	Auckland, Powerstation
23rd	Dee Why, The Venue
24-25th	Sydney, Selina's
26th	Woolongong, Waves
28th	Brisbane, Transformers
29th	Gold Coast, Playroom
May 1st	Melbourne, The Palace
2nd	Adelaide, Old Lion Hotel
3rd	Perth, Berlin Club
7th	Singapore, SLF Auditorium

Steve Garvey was by now married and living in New York, and the travel demands across the Atlantic for each tour or recording session proved impossible, exacerbated by his responsibilities to his wife and two young children. He has not played with Buzzcocks since.

Tony Barber and Phil Barker join the band, both without an audition - they are avid fans and therefore have a detailed knowledge of Buzzcocks material.

(Shelley/Diggle/Barber/Barker)

Aug 25th
Shelley, Diggle, Barber and Barker rehearse for the first time at Show Me Studio, Kentish Town. New bassist Tony Barber asks "Which of

the 57 songs do you want to play?" and then has to remind Shelley and Diggle of the tracks, as they have forgotten half of them. They continue to rehearse there daily until 5th September.

Sept 6th	Full dress rehearsal at John Henry's studio, in Camden
7th	London, Town and Country Club
20th	France, St. Quinten Festival
22nd	ITV screen *Video View* with Shelley and Diggle
Nov 18th	TV recording at LWT for *In Bed With Me Dinner*
20th	LWT screen *In Bed With Me Dinner* featuring 'What Do I Get?/Ever Fallen In Love?'
30th	Rehearsing at The Playground, London
Dec 1-2nd	Rehearsing at The Playground, London
3rd	Truro, City Hall
4th	Southampton (cancelled)
16th	Barcelona, Zeleste II
17th	Madrid, Universal- Broadcast live by Spanish Radio
18th	Valencia, Arena
19th	Basque Country, Txixarre

1993

EUROPEANTASTIC TOUR 1993

Jan 28th	Paris, Elysee Monmartre
29th	Lille, L'Aeronef
30th	Rennes, L'Ubu
31st	Brest, Les Hesperides
Feb 2nd	Tours, Le Bateau Ivre
3rd	Bordeaux, Theatre Barbey (Broadcast live on radio)
4th	Montpellier, Salle Victoire 2
5th	Auch, La Nuit
6th	Albi, C.C.A
8th	Toulouse, Salle F.M.R
9th	Villeurbanne, Le transclub
10th	Marseille, Espace Julien
12th	Reims, L'Usine
13th	Nancy, Chez Paulette
14th	Chaux-de-Fonds, Bikini Test

15th	Return to London
18th	Rehearsals begin at The Playground, London for new album *Trade Test Transmissions* (18th Feb - 8th March)

Feb 23rd-26th
Steve Diggle's solo aspirations continue at Drone Studios recording material with producer Paul Roberts, despite being actively involved in writing material with Buzzcocks. Tracks recorded include 'Heated And Rising/Over And Out/Terminal' for release on his 'Heated And Rising' solo EP.

Mar 8th
Buzzcocks sign deal with Castle Communications at Eastcote Studios in London. They begin recording the next day.

Apr 5th
Photo shoot for Castle Communications.

Apr 7th
Buzzcocks finish recording and mixing their album *Trade Test Transmissions*. The album is mastered at Exchange in London the same day.

Apr 22nd
London, Zeebra Bar - *Trade Test Transmissions* album launch. This brand new Buzzcocks album was bound to be the source of much attention, and no doubt the media knives were sharpened for the expected substandard come-back. It is all the more to the Buzzcocks' credit that the album was critically received so highly. *NME* talked of it being "a grimy follow-up to *A Different Kind Of Tension*, stuffed full of Diggle's frustrations and counterbalanced by Shelley's lovelorn yelps" whilst *Billboard* were more directly approving, saying "this is a logical fourth album that could have been released in 1981. It has all the essential ingredients for legendary status." *Melody Maker* were even more rapturous, saying "On this album, Buzzcocks sound like men at the height of their creative powers." Unfortunately, due to unforeseen distribution difficulties, this excellent album struggled to sell as well as it should have, and consequently did not chart. Nevertheless, the band set out on a mammoth world tour, consisting of an exhausting 120 dates in 12 countries over just eight months.

TRADE TEST TRANSMISSIONS UK TOUR 1993

May 4th-10th	Rehearsals at The Playground, London
11th	Kidderminster, Market Tavern
13th	Belfast, Conor Hall
14th	Dublin, Tivoli
15th	Galway, Vagabonds
18th	Guildford, Civic
19th	Rayleigh, Pink Toothbrush
20th	Cinderford, Dean Centre
21st	Portsmouth, Wedgewood Rooms
22nd	BBC Radio Five (Live Session) *Way Out Show* featuring 'Innocent/Ever Fallen In Love?/Isolation/Do It/When Love Turns Around' as well as an interview
23rd	Birmingham, Edwards No. 8
24th	Bristol, Bierkerkeller
25th	Trowbridge, Psychic Pig
26th	Nottingham, Rock City
27th	Leeds Polytechnic
28th	Tamworth, Media Centre
29th	London, The Forum
30th	Leicester, Princess Charlotte
June 1st	Sheffield, Lead Mill
2nd	Warrington, Parr Hall
3rd	Liverpool, Royal Court
4th	Manchester, University
5th	Blackburn, Windsor Suite
7th	Aberdeen, Pelican
8th	Dundee, Oscars
9th	Edinburgh, The Venue
10th	Ayr, Powerhaus
11th	Glasgow, Cat House
13th	Middlesborough, The Arena
14th	Newcastle, Riverside
15th	Blackburn, Windsor Suite
16th	Cambridge, The Junction
17th	Windsor, Old Trout
18th	Chelmsford, Anglia University
19th	Brighton, Centre East Wing
20th	Derby, Warehouse

21st	Worcester, Northwich Theatre
22nd	Newport, T.J.'s
23rd	Reading, T.U. Club
24th	Salisbury, Arts Centre
25th	Plymouth, Cooperidge
26th	London, The Grand (BBC Radio 'National Music Day')
27th	Northampton, Roadmenders Club
	BBC Radio broadcast for 'National Music Day' highlights include 'Isolation/Do It'
28th	Band receive passports for US tour

July 7th
BBC Radio Five Session (Live from Manchester) *Hit the North* featuring 'Innocent/All Over You/Isolation/Unthinkable/Do It' and a short interview

14th	London, Powerhaus
15th	Buzzcocks film video for 'Do It' at Wembley Studios,London with John Klien
16th	Stratford-upon-Avon, Phoenix Festival
21st	MTV screen 'Last To Know' recorded live at the Phoenix Festival

USA TOUR

22nd	Rochester, N.Y.
23rd	New York City
24th	Providence, Rhode Island
25th	New Haven, C.T.
26th	Washington, D.C.
Sep 1st	BBC Radio *Summer Roadshow* at Southport
2-3rd	Rehearsing at The Playground, London
4th	'Do It' video screened on ITV's *The Chart Show*

TRADE TEST TRANSMISSIONS WORLD TOUR PART 2

Sep 6th	Hamburg, Markethalle
	'Roll It Over', recorded live at the Phoenix Festival, is screened on *The Beat*
7th	Arhus, Huset
8th	Goteburg, Magasinet

9th	Stockholm, Melody
10th	Upsala, Barowiak
13th	Berlin, SO 36
14th	Hannover, Weltspiele
15th	Essen, Zeche Carl
16th	Frankfurt, Batschkapp
17th	Stuttgart, Rohre
18th	Nurnberg, Komm
19th	Munich, Terminal 1
20th	Saarbruchen, Ballhaus
22nd	Groningen, Simplon
23rd	Apeldoorn, Gigant

Buzzcocks fly in to London from Holland to perform at the launch party of the BBC book *In Session Tonight*. They appear live on the *Lunch Time Show* with Jakki Brambles, from Maida Vale Studio 5, where they play 'Ever Fallen In Love?' on air. They also perform 'Promises' for the studio audience after they go off the air. The same afternoon, they record a session for the *Johnny Walker Show* featuring 'Isolation/Do It/Unthinkable/Palm Of Your Hand', but this is not broadcast. They then return to Holland for a gig at Apeldoorn, Gigant.

24th	Den Haag, Paard
25th	Geraardbergen, Via Rock festival
26th	Haarlem, Patronaat
	Record session for VPRO Radio, Hilversum, Holland, featuring 'All Over You/Isolation/Do It/Trash/Innocent'
27th	Rotterdam, Nightown
28th	Utrecht, Tivoli
30th	Milan, Bloom
Oct 1st	Florence, Auditorium Flog
2nd	Rome, Mattatoio
4th	Vienna, Arena
6th	Marseille, Le Trolly Bus
7th	Montpellier, Victory 2
8th	Toulouse, Bikini
10th	Nancy, Chez Paulette
11th	Paris, Arapaho
2th	Amsterdam, Paradiso
14th	Liege, La Chapelle
21st	Tampere, Tulikameri
22nd	Helsinki, Tavastia

NORTH AMERICAN TOUR 1993

Nov 1st	New York, HMV
4th	Ft. Lauderdale, The Edge
5th	Tampa, Fl., Ritz Theatre
6th	Gainesville, FL., Florida Theatre
8th	Virginia Beach, VA., Richmond, Flood Zone
9th	Danbury, CT., Tuxedo Junction
10th	Philadelphia, PA., Chestnut Cabaret
11th	Boston, MA., Paradise
12th	Montreal., Club Soda
13th	Toronto., Lee's Place
14th	Buffalo, N.Y., Icon
15th	Cleveland, OH., Agora Ballroom
16th	Pittsburgh, PA., Metropol
17th	Cincinnati, OH., Bogarts
18th	Detroit, MI., Industry
19th	Chicago, IL., Metro
20th	Minneapolis, MN., First Avenue
22nd	Denver, CO., Ogden Theatre
23rd	Salt Lake City, UT., DV8
25th	Seattle, WA., RKCNDY
26th	Victoria, Canada., Harpos
27th	Vancouver, Canada., Commodore
28th	Portland, OR., La Luna
30th	Santa Cruz, CA., Catalyst
Dec 1st	Palo Alto, CA., The Edge
2nd	San Francisco, CA., Show Folks
3rd	Los Angeles, CA., The Palace
	Los Angeles, CA., The Viper Room

Tonight, Buzzcocks play two gigs. Diggle is rushed to hospital suffering from electric shock after smashing a microphone stand through one of the television sets onstage. Meanwhile, they meet Kurt Cobain at The Viper Room, (where River Phoenix suffered his fatal collapse) and the Nirvana lead singer asks them to support his band on their forthcoming European Tour.

4th	San Diego, CA., World Beat Center
6th	Phoenix, AZ., Library Cafe
7th	Santa Fe., Luna
9th	Dallas, TX., Trees

10th	Austin, TX., Liberty Lunch
11th	Houston, TX., Asylum
13th	New Orleans, LA., Tipitinas
14th	Atlanta, GA., Masquerade
15th	Knoxville., Electric Ballroom
16th	Washington D.C., 9:30 Club
17th	Providence, Rhode Island., Club Babyhead
18th	Asbury Park, NJ., Stone Pony
19th	New York., Limelight

1994

NIRVANA/BUZZCOCKS TOUR

Feb 3rd	Rehearsing at The Playground, London
6th	Cascais, The Pavilion
8th	Madrid, Pabellon del Real Madrid
9th	Barcelona, Palalio Del Los Deportes
10th	Toulouse, Palais des Sports
11th	Montpellier, Salle Victoire (Headlining)
12th	Toulon, Zenith
14th	Paris, Zenith
15th	Paris, Zenith (cancelled)
16th	Rennes, Salle Omnisports
17th	Mulhouse, Le Noumatrouf (Headlining)
18th	Grenoble, Le Summen
19th	Strasbourg, Salle de la Marseillaise (Headlining)

Mar 3rd
Pete Shelley and Tony Barber begin recording demo's for the next single 'Libertine Angel', at Barber's North London home on Shelley's 8-track machine. The demo sessions last until March 6th, followed by two additional days the following week (10th and 11th).

Mar 14-16th
Buzzcocks rehearse at The Playground, London for their next single 'Libertine Angel'.

Mar 17th-22nd
Buzzcocks record their next single 'Libertine Angel' at Falconer Studios in London.

Mar 23rd
'Libertine Angel' is mastered at Exchange in London.

Apr 1st	London, Leisure Lounge (Secret gig - onstage at 1.30am)
2nd	Recording at L.W.T. for *In Bed With Me Dinner*
11th	BBC Radio One Session (Live) for *The Mark Radcliffe Show* featuring 'Energy/Libertine Angel/Roll It Over/Last to Know'
13th	GLR Radio Session (Live) featuring 'Ever Fallen In Love?/Roll It Over' and an interview
15th	LWT transmit *In Bed With Me Dinner* featuring 'Harmony In My Head/Libertine Angel/Promises'
20th	Band view the video for 'Libertine Angel'
25-28th	Rehearsing at The Playground, London
30th	Glasgow, The Garage
May 1st	Newcastle, Riverside
2nd	Leeds, Metropolitan University
3rd	Wolverhampton, Wulfrun Hall
4th	Manchester University (Mike Joyce plays drums on the encore of 'Orgasm Addict')
5th	London, Astoria
7th	France, Brittany, St. Brieuc Salle de Robien Festival (headlining)
12th	Brighton, Hewison Hall During the day, the band shoot a photo session on Tower Bridge for an Australian music paper
13th	Bristol, Trinity Arts Centre
14th	Norwich, University of East anglia
15-16th	Oxford, The Venue
20th	Dublin, Trinity College (May Ball)
25th	Shelley appears on BBC Radio's *Antique Records Roadshow*

AUSTRALIAN AND JAPANESE TOUR

June 8th	Melbourne, Central Club
9th	Wollongong, Ocean Beach Hotel
10th	Sydney, Selina's
11th	Mooloolaba, Sunshine Hotel
12th	Gold Coast, Playroom
13th	Brisbane, The Site

14th	Adelaide, Heaven
16th	Canberra, Anu
17th	Sydney, Springfields
18th	Peakhurst, Loco's
21st	Tokyo, On Air (Broadcast live by local Radio)
23rd	Return from Australia and Japan

July 16th	Rehearsing at Playground Rehearsal Studio Windsor, Old Trout
17th	Stratford-upon-Avon, Phoenix Festival
19th	Glasgow Fair Festival

This is a Pete Shelley, solo acoustic set featuring 'Telephone Operator/Innocent/What Do I Get?/Witness The Change/Never Again/Oh Maxine/Just One Of Those Affairs/Do Anything/Give It To Me/Do It/Orgasm Addict/Everybody's Happy Nowadays/Ever Fallen In Love?/ Homosapien/Oh Shit!'

Aug 6th   London, Finsbury Park 'Madstock Festival'

Oct 17th
Granada TV transmit a 30 minute documentary on the band, called *With..... The Buzzcocks!* The programme contained footage of the band's first ever gig on silent super 8mm film, mixed with videos from the current line-up.

Dec 18th
Diggle plays a solo date at Jacksons Lane Community Centre, London.

1995

Mar 27-31st
Rehearsing at Playground, for a French tour, which will include dates due to be recorded and released on a live album in July 1995. This album will contain no new material, but will be a collection of the band's live highlights.

Apr 3rd	Ris Orangis, Le Plan
4th	Strasbourg, La Laiterie
	(Recorded live for radio broadcast)
5th	Nancy, Terminal Export
6th	Lyon, Le Glob

7th	Le-Mans, Le Royal
8th	Cahors, Chapiteau (cancelled)
	Gig moved to Rennes, Satori
9th	Bordeaux, Theatre Barbey
10th	Angers, Le Chabada
12th	Paris, Arapaho
	Recorded live by Zipper Mobile for the live album
18th	London, Camden Palace (secret gig)

The live album, provisionally titled *French*, contains the following tracks: I Don't Mind/Who Will Help Me To Forget/Get On Our Own/Unthinkable/Strange Thing/Energy/Breakdown/ Innocent/ Why She's A Girl From The Chainstore/Last To Know/Running Free/Why Can't I Touch It?/Noise Annoys /Isolation/ Boredom/ Do It/Harmony In My Head/I Believe

Apr 27th
Buzzcocks, minus Pete Shelley (who was suffering from 'flu), play a charity gig in aid of The Japanese Earthquake Fund, at London's Blue Note Club. The line-up, which features Steve Diggle, Tony Barber and Phil Barker, are joined onstage by 'Hooligan', the guitarist with These Animal Men. They perform 'Freeze' and 'Mind Blowing Groove', then Diggle performs solo for 'Game Show Host' and 'Terminal' (all four are Diggle compositions). The entire gig, featuring various other artists, is filmed for video release in Japan.

May 15-17th   Mixing live album at The Surgery, in Barnet.

27th June   Tours Mini Festival, France

20th July   Leeds Roundhay Park Festival

Summer 1995
Shelley and Diggle are writing and recording new material for a studio album, penned in for a September 1995 release, with a scheduled world tour taking in the UK, USA, Australia and Europe. With this extensive tour taking them through into 1996, Buzzcocks will then be celebrating their twentieth year in the business.

DISCOGRAPHY

For the following releases, record companies use these catalogue prefixes: UP/UA/BF/UAG - United Artists; ZS - Wizard Records; ESS - Essential Records; OG - Pickwick; ORG - New Hormones; IRS - IRS; SF - Strange Fruit; EM - EMI; PP - Planet Pacific; D/DP - Document; LBR/ATK/BP - Liberty; FA - Fame; WS - Weird Systems; FC - Fan Club; AF - Absolutely Free; RR - Receiver; RE - Roir/Danceteria; SH/SP - EMI Harvest; VCL - Virgin; Copy - Rough Trade; WIP/UWIP/XX/XS/ILP/XL - Genetic/ Island; IMMAC - Immaculate; MER - Mercury;/Phonogram; RED - Red Rhino; SIR - Sire; WEIRD - Weird Sisters; MCM - MCM; THIN - Thin Line; 330 - 3:30 Records; BB - Bent; TJM - TJM Records; BOK - Bok Bok; IVE - Illusive; IP - Imperial; CDMGRAM - Anagram

BUZZCOCKS

SINGLES

10/77	UP 36316	Orgasm Addict/What Ever Happened To?
11/77	UP 36316	What Ever Happened To ? (12" promo one side only)
02/78	UP 36348	What Do I Get?/Oh Shit!
04/78	UP 36386	I Don't Mind/Autonomy
05/78	UA LP-15	Moving Away From The Pulsebeat (12" promo one side only)
05/78	ZS12198	I Am The Amazing Buzzcocks (12" release in Australia available in clear, blue and black vinyl)
07/78	UP 36433	Love You More/Noise Annoys
09/78	UP 36455	Ever Fallen In Love?/Just Lust
11/78	UP 36471	Promises/Lipstick
03/79	UP 36499	Everybody's Happy Nowadays/Why Can't I Touch It? (3 different coloured sleeves)
07/79	UP 36541	Harmony In My Head/Something's Gone Wrong Again (red or blue picture sleeve)
09/79	BP 316	You Say You Don't Love Me/Raison D'Etre
08/80	BP 365	Why She's A Girl From The Chainstore/Are Everything (Part 1)
10/80	BP 371	Strange Thing/Airwaves Dream (Part 2)
12/80	BP 392	Running Free/What Do You Know? (Part 3)

(All of the above are on United Artists, except ZS12198 I Am The Amazing Buzzcocks, released on Wizard Records, Australia)

10/92	OG 6182	Ever Fallen In Love?/What Do I Get?/Promises
05/93	ESSX 2025	Innocent/Who'll Help Me To Forget/Inside
05/93	ESSST2025	Innocent (12")
08/93	ESSX 2031	Do It/Trash Away (live)/All Over You (live)
08/93	ESST 2031	Do It (12")
04/94	ESSX 2038	Libertine Angel/Roll It Over/excerpt from Prison Riot Hostage
04/94	ESST 2038	Libertine Angel

EP's

01/77	Org 1	Spiral Scratch (Breakdown/Times Up/Boredom/Friends Of Mine)
08/79	Org 1	Spiral Scratch (re-issue)
02/81	IRSSP70955	Parts 1-3 (US)
01/88	SFPS 044	The Peel Session (7/9/77)
10/89	CD EM104	Fab Four (Ever Fallen In Love?/Promises/Everybody's Happy Nowadays/Harmony In My Head)
10/89	12 EM 104	Fab Four (12")
10/89	EM 104	Fab Four (7")
04/91	PPAC 3CD	Alive Tonight (Alive Tonight/Serious Crime/Last To Know/Successful Street)
04/91	PPAC 3	Alive Tonight (7")
04/91	PPAC 3T	Alive Tonight (12")
09/91	DVIT	Spiral Scratch (Limited edition CD)
09/91	DVIT	Spiral Scratch (12")
09/91	DPRO-1	Spiral Scratch (7" limited promo free with *Times Up* LP re-issue)

ALBUMS

03/78	UAG 30159	**Another Music In A different Kitchen** (with limited edition carrier bag): Fast Cars/No Reply/You Tear Me Up/Get On Our Own/Love Battery/Sixteen/I Don't Mind/Fiction Romance/Autonomy/I Need/Moving Away From The Pulsebeat
03/78	UAG 30159	Another Music In A different Kitchen
09/78	UAG 30197	**Love Bites** Real World/Ever Fallen In Love?/Operators Manual/Nostalgia/Just Cut/Sixteen Again/Walking Distance/Love Is Lies/Nothing Left/ESP/Late For The Train
09/79	UAG 30260	**A Different Kind Of Tension** (with limited free single (BP 316): Paradise/Sitting 'Round At Home/You Say You Don't Love Me/You Know You Can't Help It/Mad Mad Judy/Raison D'Etre/I Don't Know What To Do With My Life/Money/Hollow Inside/A Different Kind Of Tension/I Believe/Radio Nine
11/81	LBR 1043	**Singles Going Steady** Orgasm Addict/What Do I Get?/I Don't Mind/Love You More/Ever Fallen In Love?/Promises/Everybody's Happy Nowadays/Harmony In My Head/What Ever Happened To?/Oh Shit!/Autonomy/Noise Annoys/Just Lust/Lipstick/Why Can't I Touch It?/Something's Gone Wrong Again (You Say You Don't Love Me was *not* on the album, since it was mastered for a US release, before this track was released)
08/85	ATAK 51	Another Music In A Different Kitchen
08/85	ATAK 52	Singles Going Steady

03/87	FA 3174	Love Bites
04/87	WS 021	Total Pop
06/87	FC 021	Another Music In A Different Kitchen (blue vinyl)
06/87	FC 022	Love Bites (blue vinyl)
06/87	FC 023	A Different Kind Of Tension (blue Vinyl)
05/88	CDFA 3199	Another Music In A Different Kitchen
05/88	FA 3199	Another Music In A Different Kitchen
05/88	CDFA 3174	Love Bites
06/88	EMI CZ 93	A Different Kind Of Tension
09/89	AFCD002	**Live At The Roxy Club April 1977**
09/89	AFLP002	Live At The Roxy Club April 1977
02/90	SFRCD104	**The Peel Sessions Album**
02/90	SFRLP104	The Peel Sessions Album
06/90	RRLP 131	Live At The Roxy
03/91	RRCD 131	Live At The Roxy
10/90	FA 3241	Singles Going Steady
10/90	CDFA 3241	Singles Going Steady
08/91	DLP2	**Times Up** (free interview flexi)
08/91	DCD2	Times Up
10/91	EMI CDEM 1421	**Operators Manual** (Hits compilation)
02/92	EMI CDP 7987292	**Entertaining Friends** (Recorded live at Hammersmith Odeon March 31/3/79)
04/93	RE158CD	**Lest We Forget** (Import compilation live album of 1979/80 American Tour)
05/93	ESSCD195	**Trade Test Transmissions** Do It/Innocent/T.T.T./Isolation/Smile/Last To Know/ When Love Turns Around/never Gonna Give It Up/ Energy/Palm Of Your Hand/Alive Tonight/Who Will Help Me To Forget/Unthinkable/Crystal Night/369
05/93	ESSLP195	Trade Test Transmissions
04/94	EMI CDPRDT 12	Another Music In A Different Kitchen/Love Bites (both albums on one CD)
05/94	SFRCD104	The Peel Album (Re-issue/different sleeve)

BOX SETS

10/89	EMI CD PRDT 1	**Product** (3 CD set; Re-issued 6/95)
10/89	EMI LP PRDT 1	Product (LP set)

Both feature all the albums, plus a bonus album, with Side 1 featuring Capital Radio's Live from London's Lyceum broadcast on 10/3/78 including Brekdown/Fast Cars/Noise Annoys/Pulsebeat/Fiction Romance/What Do I get?/What Ever Hppened To?/Times Up and Side 2 including Are Everything/Strange Thing/What Do You Know?/Why She's A Girl From The Chainstore/Airwaves Dream/Running Free and a bonus track, I Look Alone (previously unreleased on vinyl)

COMPILATION ALBUMS

07/77	SHSP 4069	The Roxy Club, London WC2
		(features Breakdown and Love Battery)
06/78	VCL 5003	Short Circuit At The Electric Circus
		(features Times Up)(later re-issued on CD)
02/81	Copy 001	C81 (Various Artists)
		(features I Look Alone - originally intended as Part 4)
		(available on cassette only)
06/92	CDVCL 5003	Short Circuit At The Electric Circus
		(re-issued of above vinyl)
09/93	Book CD-1	In Session Tonight (Various Artists)
		(strictly limited edition BBC session recordings available free with the book of the same title. Apart from The Cure, Undertones, Billy Bragg and others the CD contains What Do I Get? from John Peel session 9/77)

BUZZCOCKS RARITIES

Bootleg audience recordings exist of many Buzzcocks concerts and as such, sound quality varies from very good to unlistenable. Despite this, Buzzcocks bootlegs remain very collectable. Only those of historical importance or rarity value are listed below:

Jets Of Air, Naylor's Farm/Davies' house September 1973
Telephone Operator/Editions of You/Hang On To Yourself/Remake Remodel/ White Light, White Heat/Back In The USSR/Jean Jeanie/John, I'm Only Dancing/Queen Bitch/Suffragette City/I Just Can't Live

Screen On The Green, London 29/8/76
Breakdown/Friends Of Mine/Times Up/Orgasm Addict/Peking Hooligan (unrecorded Devoto composition)/Lester Sands/Oh Shit!/Tear Me Up/Love Battery/I Can't Control Myself

Buzzcocks United Artists, First Demo Tape
Orgasm Addict/What Do I Get?/What Ever Happened To? Recorded at Arrow Studios, Manchester, 31/8/77, with Davies on bass

Steve Diggle, 'Fourth album', demo's
Can You Dig It/Drift Away/Back Of My Mind/Dancing At Dawn/By MySide/ Don't Come Back. These were recorded at Diggle's home on a portastudio, and actually not intended for any album. Until recently, Diggle himself did not have these recordings, until a sympathetic fan sent him a copy.

Drone Studio Session 21-24/11/80
Dreaming/Alive Tonight/Never Gonna Give It Up/Wallpaper World/Successful Street/Who Will Help Me To Forget/Serious Crime/Why Compromise?

Drone Studio Session 13/2-24/4/91
Never Gonna Give It Up/Serious Crime/Dreaming/Last To Know/Run Away
From Home/Tranquiliser/Alive Tonight/Love Turns Around You/Isolation/
Successful Street/Who Will Help Me To Forget/Run Away From Home//Australia

The Unreleased Album 1991
Isolation/Never Gonna Give It Up/When Love Turns Around/All Over
You/Trash Away/Who Will Help Me To Forget/Run Away From Home/Why
Compromise?/Alive Tonight/Last To Know/Insider/Serious Crime/Tranquiliser.
Recorded at Green Point Studio New York, 9-22/12/91 with Bill Laswell.

PETE SHELLEY SOLO DISCOGRAPHY

SINGLES/EP's

03/80   ORG 3   Big Noise From The Jungle EP with Tiller Boys line-up of Pete
Shelley (guitar) Eric Random (guitar) and Francis Cookson (drums)featuring Big
Noise From The Jungle/Slaves And Pyramids/What Me, Worry? (7" instrumentals)

09/81	WIP 6720	Homosapien/Keat's Song (7")
06/82	WIP 6720	Homosapien/Love In Van
		(Re-issue with different B side)
06/82	12WIP 6720	Homosapien(Dance Version)/Homosapien
		(12" dancepartydubmix)
11/81	UWIP 6740	I Don't Know What It Is/Witness The Change
		(Double Pack with free single - In Love With Somebody
		Else/Maxine)
11/81	12WIP 6740	I Don't Know What It Is(remix)/Witness The Change/I
		Don't Know What It Is (instrumental version)
03/82	NSNS-1	Qu'est-ce C'est Que Ca/Amor (7")
		(free yellow flexi-disc with issue 9 of *New Sounds, New*
		Style magazine - Side 2 by Animal Magnet - not Shelley)
03/83	XX1	Telephone Operator/Many A Time (7")
03/83	12XX1	Telephone Operator/Many A Time (Extended)/Many A
		Time (12" dub mix)
05/83	XS2	(Millions Of People)No One Like You/If You Ask Me I
		Won't Say No (7")
05/83	12XS2	(Millions Of People)No One Like You/If You Ask Me I
		Won't Say No (12" dub mix)
11/84	IMMAC1	Never Again/One One One
11/84	12IMMAC 1	Never Again (Extended version)/Give It To Me/One
		One One (12" Extended version)
02/86	MER215	Waiting For Love/Designer Lamps (7")
02/86	MERX215	Waiting For Love(Extended Version)/Waiting For Love
		(7" version) (12")
00/88	12IMMAC 4	Waiting For Love (Immaculate Mix One)/Waiting For
		Love (7" version)/Designer Lamps (12")

05/86	MER 221	On Your Own/Please Forgive Me.... But I Cannot Endure It Any Longer (7")
05/86	MER 4228847511	On Your Own(New York remix)/On Your Own (New York dub)/Please Forgive Me.... But I Cannot Endure It Any Longer (Extended version) (12")
05/86	MERX 221	On Your Own(New York remix)/On your Own (Dub Mix)/Please Forgive Me.... But I Cannot Endure It Any Longer (12")
07/86	MER 225	Blue Eyes/Nelson's Riddle (excerpt) (7")
07/86	MERX225	Blue Eyes (Extended version)/Nelson's Riddle (12")
11/86	MER 234	I Surrender/ Need a Minit (7")
11/86	MERX234	I Surrender(UK remix version)/I Surrender (Dub Mix)/Need A Minit (12")
05/88	IMMAC5	Your Love/Give It To Me (7")

05/88 IMMAC5 — Recorded by a three piece called Zip, formed by Pete Shelley (guitar/vocals), with Gerard Cookson on guitar/programing and Mark Sanderson on bass guitar. This was their one and only release. The instrumental riff from 'Your Love' is featured as the theme music for Channel 4's *Tour de France* programme.

05/88	12IMMAC5	Your Love/Your Love(extended version)/Give It To Me(extended version) (12")
04/89	IMMAC11	Homosapien II/Homosapien II(instrumental)
04/89	12IMMAC11	Homosapien II(Icon mix)/ Homosapien II(Techno mix) (12")
04/89	IMMAC11CD	Homosapien II/Homosapien II(Icon mix)/ Homosapien II(radio mix)/Homosapien II(shower mix/no vocals

ALBUMS

01/82 ILPS 9676   Homosapien
Recorded at Genetic Studios, Berkshire
Line Up: Pete Shelley - guitars/vocals; Martin Rushent - bass/programming

07/83 XL1   XL-1
Line Up: Pete Shelley - guitar/vocals; Barry Adamson - bass; Jim Russell - drums; Martin Rushent - keyboards. Recorded at Genetic Studios, Berks. This album features a Sinclair ZX Spectrum computer code which prints lyrics in time with the music.

06/86 MERH90   Heaven And The Sea
Line Up: Pete Shelley - guitar/vocals; Gerard Cookson - guitars; Jack Lambert - bass; James Gardiner - keyboards; Dave Beebee - drums. Recorded at Synchro Soound and Park Avenue Studios, Boston. Completed at Strong Room Studio, Mayfair Studio and Advisions Studios,

06/86 MERHC90   Heaven And The Sea

08/87 MCF 3365   Some Kind Of Wonderful (Various Artists)
(1987 soundtrack - Shelley wrote and sings 'Do Anything')

08/88	RED-CD-88	Till Things Get Brighter (Various Artists) (Johnny Cash tribute album in aid of the Terence Higgins Trust. Shelley sings 'Straight A's In Love')
02/90	MCAD 6200	Some Kind Of Wonderful (Various Artists (Re-issue on CD - see above)
09/92	830 004-2	Heaven And The Sea (re-issue with three bonus tracks)
09/94	GRACD 201	Homosapien (re-issue with six bonus tracks)
09/94	GRACD 202	XL-1 (re-issue with four bonus tracks)

In 1979, Pete Shelley and Francis Cookson set up their own label called Groovy Records. The label released the following albums:

01/80	Groovy STP 1	£3.33p/Free Agents (Tiller Boys, Eric Random and Francis Cookson recorded live at York University, August 1978 and studio tracks recorded at Graveyard Studios, Prestwich with Pete Shelley, Eric, Francis and Allan (vocalist with The Worst)
04/80	Groovy STP 2	Sky Yen (Parts 1 & 2) (Sleeve notes read "Performed on a purpose built oscillator", March 1974
08/80	Groovy STP 3	Hangahar (Soundtrack to a surrealistic film Pete became involved in with Sally Smmitt and Lindsay Lee.)

GUEST APPEARANCES

Fellow Manchester artist John Cooper-Clarke had featured with Buzzcocks during 1977 on several occasions as the supporting act. Pete Shelley featured on the following John Cooper-Clarke releases:

11/78	CBS 83132	John Cooper-Clarke: Disguise In Love (LP) (Shelley plays guitar on three tracks - Teenage Werewolf /(I Married A)Monster From Outer Space/Strange Bedfellows
05/80	EPIC 84083	John Cooper-Clarke: Snap, Crackle And Bop (LP) (Shelley plays guitar on the single from the album *Thirty Six Hours*)
05/80	EPIC SEPC 8655	John Cooper-Clarke: Thirty Six Hours/It Man (7") (Shelley plays guitar on Thirty Six Hours)
06/78	V2100	Magazine: Real Life (LP) (features 'Shot By Both Sides' and 'The Light Pours Out Of Me', both co-written with Shelley)

PETE SHELLEY RARITIES

Audience recordings exist of the following Pete Shelley gigs: Brixton Fridge 21/12/81 (solo debut); Brixton Fridge 29/12/81; Edinburgh, Valentino's 8/3/82/Glasgow; Maestro's 7/4/82; New York, Ritz 17/4/82; Canada, Concordia

University 19/4/82; San Diego, Bacchanal 6/5/82; Philadelphia, Ripely Hall 26/5/82; New York, My Fathers Place 30/5/82; Glasgow College 22/6/84; Leeds University 27/6/84; Glastonbury, Elephant Fayre 28/7/84; Edinburgh, Coasters 14/3/85; Manchester, Hacienda 27/3/85; Leeds, Warehouse 30/4/86; Manchester, International 1/5/86; Brighton, Pavillion 8/5/86; London, Electric Ballroom 14/5/86; Manchester, G-Mex 19/7/86; London, Finsbury Park 27/7/86; Brighton, Zap Club 7/11/86; Kingston Poly 8/11/86; Croydon, Underground 9/11/86; London University 14/11/86; Blackburn, Windsor Suite 29/11/86; Salford University 6/11/87; London Polytechnic 11/12/87;

Apart from the audience recordings listed above the following is a list of Pete Shelley's most interesting recordings:

BBC Radio 1 - *Kid Jensen Show*, broadcast: 21/12/81 Performs 'I Generate A Feeling/ Witness The Change/Yesterday's Not Here'
Line Up: Pete Shelley - guitar/vocals; Barry Adamson - bass; Alan Dalgleish - keyboards

BBC Radio 1 - *Rock On*, Richard Skinner, broadcast: 27/3/82 Interview

BBC Radio 1 - *Kid Jensen Show*, broadcast: 14/2/83 Performs 'Many A Time/ Telephone Operator/I Just Want To Touch'
Line Up: Pete Shelley - Guitar/vocals; Barry Adamson - bass; Gerard Cookson - guitar; Mel Wesson - keyboards; Jim Russell - drums

BBC Radio 1 - *Rock On*, Richard Skinner, broadcast: 25/6/83 Interview

BBC Radio 1 - *Janice Long Show*, broadcast: 2/7/83 Performs 'If You Ask Me I Won't Say No/What Was Heaven?/You And I/XL-1'
Line Up: Pete Shelley - guitar; Barry Adamson - bass; Gerard Cookson - guitar; Mel Wesson - keyboards; Jim Russell - drums

BBC Radio 1 - *Janice Long Show* , broadcast: 3/10/84 Performs 'Never Again/ Waiting For Love/Life Without Reason/Give It To Me'
Line Up: Pete Shelley - guitar/vocals Barry Adamson - bass; Gerard Cookson - guitar; Jim Russell - drums (Francis Cookson is also credited on this session)

Picadilly Radio - *The Last Radio Show*, broadcast: 16/5/85 Performs 'Sixteen Again/ Ever Fallen In Love?/Homosapien/If You Ask Me I Won't Say No/What Do I Get?' (Solo acoustic session)

BBC Radio 1 - *Janice Long Show*, broadcast: 26/2/86 Performs 'I Surrender/Blue Eyes/They're Coming For You/ On Your Own'
Line Up: Pete Shelley - guitar/vocals; Peter Thomas - bass; Gerard Cookson - guitar; Norman Fisher-Jones - guitar; Jim Gardener - keyboards; Simon Hoare - drums

Picadilly Radio - *City to City*, broadcast: 25/10/86 Interview
BBC Radio 1 - *Liz Kershaw Show*, broadcast: 16/5/88 Performs 'I'm Never Gonna

Give It Up/Serious Crime/The Way You Are Is Not The Way You Were/Why Compromise?' and is interviewed
Line Up: Pete Shelley - guitar/vocals; Gerard Cookson - guitar and programming; Mark Sanderson - bass; (this is Shelley's new three piece known as Zip)

RTE Radio (Ireland) - *Dave Fanning Show*, broadcast: 27/7/88 Interview as Zip

STEVE DIGGLE & FLAG OF CONVENIENCE
SOLO DISCOGRAPHY

SINGLES/EPs

02/81	BP 389	Steve Diggle: Fifty Years Of Comparative Wealth EP: Shut Out The Light/Fifty Years Of Comparative Wealth/Here Comes The Fire Brigade) (7") Line Up: Diggle - gtr/vocs/keyboard; Steve Garvey - bass; John Maher - drums
09/82	SIR 4057	Flag Of Convenience Life On The Telephone/The Other Man's Sin (7") Available in US on 12" with two additional tracks: Picking Up On Audio Sound/Life On The Telephone (edited version) Line Up: Steve Diggle - guitar/vocals; Dave Farrow - bass; D.P. (Dave Prescot) - keyboards; John Maher - drums
03/83	WEIRD1	Change/Longest Life (7") Line Up: Steve Diggle - guitar/vocals; Gary Hamer - bass; Mark Burke - guitar; John Maher - drums
04/86	MCM 186	New House/Keep On Pushing (Keep On Pushing recorded live at Dingwalls, London 10/01/86) 7" Line Up: Steve Diggle - guitar/vocals; Gary Hamer - bass; Steve Mac - guitar; Dean Sumner - keyboards; Mac - Sax; John Caine - drums
04/87	FOC 1	Last Train To Safety EP Last Train To Safety/The Rain In England/ Human Jungle (12") Line Up: Steve Diggle - guitar/vocals; Gary Hamer - bass; John Caine - drums;
10/87	MCM 001	Should I Ever Go Deaf EP Should I Ever Go Deaf/Pictures In My Mind/Drowned In Your Heartache/The Greatest Sin (12") Line Up: Steve Diggle - guitar/vocals; Gary Hamer - bass; John Caine - drums
08/88	MCM 002	Exiles EP Exiles/Can't Stop The World/Shot Down With Your Gun/Tragedy In Market Street (12") Line Up: Steve Diggle - guitar/vocals; Gaz Conner - guitar; Gary Hamer - bass; Chris Goodwin - drums

07/89	THIN003	Buzzcocks FOC

Sunset/Life With The Lions/Sunset (Bat mix) (12")
Line Up: Steve Diggle - guitar/vocals; Gary Hamer -
bass/vocals; Andy Couzens - guitar/vocals; Chris
Goodwin - drums

09/93	330001	Steve Diggle: Heated And Rising EP

Heated & Rising/Over & Out/Terminal/Wednesday's
Flowers
Line Up: Steve Diggle - guitars/vocals; Ken Heggie -
bass; Steve Gibson - drum. Recorded at Drone Studios.

ALBUMS

09/83	FAN 1	The Big Secret (Cassette Only)

Line Up: Steve Diggle - guitars/vocals; Dave Farrow -
bass; Gary Hamer - bass; John Maher - drums. Recorded
at Cargo Studios, Rochdale

09/87	MCM010	Northwest Skyline

Line Up: Steve Diggle - Guitar/vocals; Gary Hamer -
bass; John Caine - drums; John Maher - drums (2 tracks
only). Recorded at Twilight Studios, Salford

03/88	MCM 020	War On The Wireless Set (US Only)

Line Up: Steve Diggle - Guitar/vocals; Gary Hamer -
bass; Steve Garvey - bass (two tracks only); John Maher -
drums. Recorded at Revolution Studios, Stockport
andCargo Studios, Rochdale, this is a compilation of
Flag Of Convenience out-takes from 1981-86.

02/94	CDMGRAM 74	The Best Of Steve Diggle And Flag Of Convenience

The Secret Public Years1981-1989

DIGGLE RARITIES

Audience recordings exist of the following Flag Of Convenience gigs:
Wolverhampton, Polytechnic 8/10/82;London, Marquee 20/3/83; Camden,
Dingwalls 8/4/85; London, Marquee 11/8/85; London, Marquee 5/10/85;
Kennington Oval Cricketers 14/10/85; London, Dingwalls 10/1/86; Kentish Town,
Bull and Gate 22/1/86; London, Dingwalls 7/3/86; Clarendon Broadway 2/7/87;
Fulham, Greyhound 24/9/87; London, Robey 28/1/88; London, Robey 6/4/88;

Apart from the audience recordings listed above the following is a list of Steve
Diggle and Flag Of Convenience's most interesting recordings:

Flag Of Convenience - 1981 Demo's
Original three piece line-up featuring Dave Farrow on bass guitar and John Maher
on drums. Tracks are Life On The Telephone/In The Back/Drift Away/Picking Up
On Audio Sound/Life On The Telephone (version 2).

Flag Of Convenience - Live at Brighton, Sherry's 22/9/82
Tracks: In The Back/Men From The City/Audio Sound/Life On The Telephone

/Drift Away/Who Is Innocent/The Accused/50 Years Of Comparative Wealth/Other Man's Sin/Shut Out The Light

Steve Diggle - Picadilly Radio 21/7/85
Tracks: The Big Secret/Harmony In My Head (solo acoustic session)

Flag Of Convenience - Live at Dingwalls, London 10/1/86
Tracks: New House/A Dance (later called 'Trash Away')/People's Pages/Are You In Heaven?/Love Has The Power/The Big Secret/What Am I Supposed To Do Now/People Stand By/Who Is Innocent/Harmony In My Head/Keep On Pushing (Last track available on New House single)

F.O.C. - Live at 'The Festival of the Tenth Summer', Manchester 19/7/86
Tracks: Last Train To Safety/The Rain In England/Harmony In My Head

BUZZCOCKS F.O.C. - Live in Halifax, England 20/8/89 (Benefit for C.A.R.E (Conservation for Rainforests and Elephants)
Tracks: Fall Out Line/Return To Reality/Forever/Wallpaper World/Sunset
(This is possibly Steve Diggle's last ever gig as a solo artist before Buzzcocks reformed)

STEVE GARVEY SOLO DISCOGRAPHY

SINGLES/EP's

01/79	BB3	The Teardrops -In A Out Of Fashion EP (12") Line up: Steve Garvey/Tony Friel/Karl Burns and various friends
07/79	TJM-7	Seeing Double/Teardrops And Heartaches (7")
05/80	BBok 2	Bok Bok - Come Back To Me/Misfit (7") (The band Bok Bok are The Teardrops)
01/80	Illuminated JAMS 2	Final Vinyl (LP) Line Up: Dave Price - vocals; Steve Garvey - guitars; Karl Burns - drums

JOHN MAHER SOLO DISCOGRAPHY

Although Maher toured with Liverpool bands Wah! and Hambi And The Dance, he did not feature on any of their recorded material. He did however, perform on one BBC Radio broadcast with Wah!. Apart from his contributions to Diggle's Flag Of Convenience, Maher also guested on the following releases:

SINGLES

08/80	IVE 1	Pauline Murray & The Invisible Girls Dream Sequences 1 & 2 (7")

11/80	IP 4301	The Things - Pieces Of You (7")
		Line Up: Tim Lyons - vocals; Dave Holmes - guitar
		vocals; Joe Brehony - bass; Ella Matcalfe - keyboards;
		John Maher - drums
04/81	IVE 3	Pauline Murray & The Invisible Girls
		Searching For Heaven/Animal Crazy (7")
04/81	IVEX 3	Searching For Heaven/Animal Crazy/Visitor
		(additional track) (12")

ALBUMS

09/80	Dreamland 2394277	Pauline Murray & The Invisible Girls
		(eponymous)
		Line Up: Pauline Murray - vocals; Dave
		Rowbotham - guitar; Vinney Reilly - guitar;
		Robert Blamire - bass; Steve Hopkins -
		keyboards; John Maher - drums;
07/79	Small Wonder 2383533	Partick Fitzgerald -Grubby Stories
		Line Up: Patrick Fitzgerald - guitar/vocals;
		Robert Blamire - bass; Maher - drums
03/79	Small Wonder 2383533	Partick Fitzgerald -Grubby Stories

NEW HORMONES DISCOGRAPHY

Although the New Hormones office in Manchester was a base for Buzzcocks' business affairs, it was also home to its own record label, set up after the success of the re-issued 'Spiral Scratch' EP, developing into a forum for various unsigned Manchester bands. Listed below is the complete New Hormones catalogue of releases, cassettes and literature:

01/77	Org 1	Buzzcocks	Spiral Scratch EP
12/77	Org 2	Linder/Savage	The Secret Public (A3 collage)
03/80	Org3	The Tiller Boys	Big Noise From The Jungle (7" EP)
03/80	Org 4	Ludus	The Visit (12")
07/80	Org 5	The Decorators	Twilight View/Reflections (7")
09/80	Org 6	Eric Random	That's What I Like About Me (12")
07/81	Org 7	Dislocation Dance	Perfectly In Control (7" EP)
07/81	Org 8	Ludus	My Cherry Is In Sherry/Anatomy Is
			Not Destiny
07/81	Org 9	Diagram Brothers	Bricks/Postal Bargains (7")
07/81	Org 10	Dislocation Dance	Slip That Disc (12")
05/81	Org 11	Eric Random	Dow Chemical Co./Skin Deep (7")
07/81	Org 12	Ludus	Mother's Hour/Patient (7")
07/81	Org 14	God's Gift	God's Gift (12" EP)
07/81	Org 15	Dislocation Dance	Music, Music, Music (LP)
09/81	Org 16	Ludus	The Seduction (2x12" LP)
11/81	Org 17	Diagram Brothers	Some Marvels Of Modern Science (LP)
03/82	Org 18	Eric Random	Earth Bound (LP)

06/82	Org 19	Dislocation Dance	Rosemary/Shake (7")
09/82	Org 20	Ludus	Danger Came Smiling (LP)
07/82	Org 21	Diagram Brothers	Discordo (10" EP)
10/82	Org 22	Dislocation Dance	You'll Never Know/You Can Tell (7")
10/82	Org 25	God's Gift	Discipline/Then Calm Again (7")
10/82	Org 30	Albertos Y Los Trios Paranoias	Cruising With Santa (7") (Christmas CND Benefit release)

In 1981, New Hormones released a series of three limited edition cassettes (500) which came with a booklet, badge, stickers and a sweatshirt offer. The cassettes had their own catalogue numbers:

07/81	Cat 1	Ludus	Pickpocket
08/91	Cat 2	C.P.Lee Mystery Guild	Radio Sweat
09/81	Cat 3	Biting Tongues	Live It

In 1982, plans for various projects and releases fell through despite catalogue numbers having been issued. From its inception, Ludus was automatically assigned all multiples of 4, and her departure thus explains the lack of Org 24 and Org 28. Org 23 was scheduled to be a cassette/calendar depicting famous assassinations with sound and pictures by Liverpudlian Ambrose Reynolds, but this was also scrapped. Finally, nobody wanted unlucky Org 13.

BOOTLEGS

1977	Voto Records LYN 5333	Times Up: Oct '76 demo's (vinyl)
1978	Edible GF 001	Best In Good Food Live tracks/TV and radio broadcasts
1979	EGGGB-9	Razor Cuts: Live tracks/demo's/TV and radio performances (clear vinyl)
1980	New Hormones SFR007	Gifts Of Love Four live tracks from Club 57, New York Sept 1st, 1979. Stamped "Fan-Club Record" - clearly a bootleg (7" EP)
1992	DIYE-CD2	Times Up CD re-issue of Times Up and Razor Cuts bootleg albums
1992	Brand New Beat 911003	Noise Annoys WNEW Radio broadcast of concert at Palladium, New York Dec 1st, 1979 (CD)
1992	Jumpin' Jive JJ002	Moving Away From The Pulsebeat, exact duplicate of Noise Annoys
1994	Hand Made HAM014	The Legendary Buzzcocks WPIX-FM broadcast of concert at Club 57, New York Sept 1st, 1979 (CD - also available on vinyl)
1995	Times Up-Shell 1	Screen On The Green (7" red vinyl) Orgasm Addict/Peking Hooligan/Lester Sands/Oh Shit! - Recorded live at Screen On The Green, Islington 29/8/76 - limited pressing of 500

VIDEOGRAPHY

16/8/77		What Do I Get? Live at Manchester's Electric Circus
27/7/78		B'dum B'dum Granada TV Special featuring Buzzcocks and Magazine screened
14/11/78		The Old Grey Whistle Test, Sixteen Again/Nothing Left Sixteen Again/Nothing Left,
6/3/79		Follies, Belgian TV, Love You More
8/3/79		Rock Pop , German TV, Everybody's Happy Nowadays
7/9/79		Interview/What Do I Get? (Live in Toronto), Canadian TV
30/8/80		Fun Factory , Granada TV, Are Everything
25/3/83		Switch Channel 4, Telephone Operator (Live)
8/7/83		Switch Channel 4, XL-1/If You Ask Me I Won't Say No (Live)
26/2/85		The Old Grey Whistle Test, Sixteen Again (repeat) with interview
11/88	K7 002	Best of Berlin Independence Days '88 Volume One: Various artists recorded live Oct 10th-12th 1988. Features Watching America by Buzzcocks FOC
03/89	K7 004	Best of Berlin Independence Days '88 Volume Two: Various artists recorded live Oct 10th-12th, 1988. Features Isolation/Tomorrow's Sunset/Watching America by Buzzcocks FOC
20/8/89		C.A.R.E. (Conservation for Rainforests and Elephants) Benefit Concert, Halifax, featuring Buzzcocks FOC, Fall Out Of Line/ Return To Reality, screened on late night UK TV
11/89	IKON 40	Auf Wiedersehen: Last performance of this line-up before split. Recorded in Hamburg, 01/81

9/12/89 Live at Brixton Academy - I Don't Know What To Do With My Life/I Don't Mind/Love You More/Promises/Why She's A Girl From The Chainstore/ Autonomy/Nothing Left/Moving Away From The Pulsebeat/Noise Annoys/You Say You Don't Love Me/E.S.P./Walking Distance/Why Can't I Touch It?/ Everybody's Happy Nowadays/Harmony In My Head/What Do You Know/What Do I Get?/Fast Cars/Ever Fallen In Love?/I Believe/Oh Shit!/Orgasm Addict/Boredom/ (Bootleg).

3/2/90		Countdown Australian TV, Ever Fallen In Love? (Live)
08/90	Castle CMP 6001	Live Legends: Recorded at Central TV Studios, Nottingham 12/89. Originally broadcast on late night music programme *Bedrock*. (Also available on Laser Disc-ID8665CA)

25/8/90 Live at the Reading Festival - Wallpaper World/Never Gonna Giv It Up/Autonomy/Nothing Left/Successful Street/Everybody's Happy Nowadays/Harmony In My Head/Ever Fallen In Love?/I Believe/Orgasm Addict /Mad Mad Judy/Boredom (Bootleg)

13/6/91	First Night, Central TV, Last To Know and Interview
7/9/92	Concert at Town and Country Club, London in aid of The Spastics Society in conjunction with *NME*: Via 8 - Real World(intro)/Fast Cars/Who'll Help Me To Forget/Last To Know/Get On Our Own/When Love Turns Around/Why Compromise/Trash Away/Noise Annoys/ Harmony In My

		Head / Sixteen / Autonomy / Inside / What Do I Get? / Orgasm Addict - Filmed and screened by Central TV
09/92	PMI MVP4910243	Playback:Promo clips, *Top of the Pops* footage, live tracks and interviews with Pete Shelley and Steve Diggle
22/9/92		Video View, Interview with Shelley / Diggle and review of Playback video
10/92	Warner 4509 91011-3	Punk: Various artists from punk era - Sex Pistols, The Jam, the Clash and many others including Buzzcocks. Live performances of 'What Do I Get? (with Garth on bass) / I Don't Mind / Love You More / Ever Fallen In Love?'
20/11/92		In Bed with Me Dinner, LWT, What Do I Get? / Ever Fallen In Love?
21/8/93		MTV / Live at Phoenix Festival, Interview / Last To Know
4/9/93		The Chart Show, Do It (Promo)
17/7/94		The Beat, Live from Phoenix Festival, Running Free
17/6/94		Cue The Music presented by Mike Mansfield, Pete Shelley Live at the Camden Palace, London May 1986, Waiting For Love / On Your Own / Never Again / My Dreams / Blue Eyes / If You Ask Me I Won't Say No / No Moon / Telephone Operator / Homosapien / Something's Gone Wrong Again
15/4/94		In Bed with Me Dinner, LWT, Harmony In My Head / Libertine Angel / Promises
6/9/94		The Beat, Live from Phoenix Festival, Roll It Over
17/10/94		*With.....The Buzzcocks* , thirty minute Granada TV Special containing footage of Buzzcocks first ever gig, promo video's and interviews

Promotional videos were filmed for the following tracks: What Do I Get? / Moving Away From The Pulsebeat / Promises / Lipstick / Why She's A Girl From The Chainstore / Homosapien / Homosapien II / Alive Tonight / Do It / Libertine Angel /

Buzzcocks appeared on *Top Of The Pops* , (often more than once for each release) for the following tracks I Don't Mind / Love You More / Ever Fallen In Love? / Promises / Everybody's Happy Nowadays / Harmony In My Head /

Apart from Revolution and Indigo Sound Studios (both used in 1976), Buzzcocks used the following studios 1977-81: Abbey Road Studios, London; Advision Studios, London; Air Studios, London; Arrow Studios, Manchester; Cargo Studios, Rochdale; Central Studios, Manchester; Drone Studios, Manchester; Eden Studios, London; Genetic Studios, Berks; Morgan Studios, London; Olympic Studios, London; Pluto Studios, Cheshire; Strawberry Studios, Stockport; Townhouse Studios, London; T.W. Studios, Fulham; Wessex Sound Studios, London.

BUZZCOCKS ON THE ROAD

1977-1981

Richard Boon (Manager), Pete Monks (Tour Manager/driver), Keith Wilde (P.A. mix), Tony Wall (P.A. monitor mix), Mike Nolan (On stage sound), Martin Mulligan (Lighting technician), Ron Clarke (Lighting), Dermot O'Meara (Drum roadie), Kristy Pollard (Back Line/mics), Chris Tervit (P.A. assistant), Franny Taylor (Roadie), Eric Ramsden (Roadie), Sarge (Personal Security)

1989-95

Raf Edmonds (Manager), Paul O'Reilly (Tour Manager 89-90), Tony Selinger (Tour Manager 90-91), Stewart James (Tour Manager 91-92), Frank Simon (Tour Manager 92-93), Andy Bernstein (Tour Manager 93-), Tim Scott (P.A. system), Mick Tyas (P.A. system), Louise Stickland (Lighting), 'Supermick' (Lee Shelley, Drum roadie 89-90), Viv Cook (Driver), Glen Power (Lighting), Sammi Hanyes (Guitar roadie), Ken Klein (Back line), Nigel Banks (Guitars/backline, Adam Berlyne (Lighting designer), John Langan (Sound), Peter Towndrow (Back line), Peter Jones (Roadie (part-time)), Greg Tinson (Driver)

THE SECRET PUBLIC

In August 1978, New Hormones set up an official fan club. For a fee of £1.50, subscribers received a fan club membership card, regular information, photographs, T-shirts, badges and special features on the band. Randomly selected members received postcard sized black and white photo's of the band, all of which became instant collectors items. Twenty eight official Buzzcocks badges were produced, each with a different theme and as membership increased the fan club official newsletter *The Secret Public* was born. Using the muted 'post-horn' symbol, the newsletter ran until March 1981 when Issue 9 announced the news that Pete had decided to leave the band. It reproduced the letter from his solicitor announcing the split, dated 4th March 1981, inside.

BIBLIOGRAPHY

Caroline Coon: *1988: The New Wave Punk Rock Explosion* (Orbach & Chambers 1977/Omnibus Press 1982)
Lee Wood: *Sex Pistols, Day By Day* (Omnibus Press, 1989)
Jon Savage: *Product* (EMI Records, 1989)
Jon Savage: *England's Dreaming - Sex Pistols And Punk Rock* (Faber and Faber, 1991)
Ken Garner: *In Session Tonight* (BBC Books, 1993)

The many magazines and fanzines.....
Time Out, New Manchester Review, The Secret Public (Linder/Jon Savage), Sniffin' Glue, Kids Stuff, The Big Take-Over, Ghast Up, God Is A Newt, City Life, City Fun, Secret Public Fan Club Newsletters, Zig Zag, Sublime (Manchester Music and Design), Late for the Real World, Harmony In My Head, Record Collector, Spiral Scratch, Q, Guitarist, and Select.

A must for the fanatical Buzzcocks fans are the following articles and interviews from the music press of the period:

"Sex Pistols/Slaughter & The Dogs/Buzzcocks live" Buzzcocks debut gig with Pistols in *Sounds* 31/7/76)

"Parade of the Punks" Two-page special *Melody Maker* 2/10/76)

"Teen Rebel scores £250 from Dad" One page feature *NME* 5/2/77

"What Ever Happened to The Buzzcocks?" Two page feature and interview with Buzzcocks and Garth *Sounds* 17/9/77

"Cocks of the North" Interview with Buzzcocks and Garth, *Record Mirror* 17/9/77

"United We Stand...." Feature on Manchester scene, *Melody Maker* 22/10/77

"Another Music From A Different Kitchen" Two-page interview *NME* 3/12/77

"Cocks Of The North" Interview with Buzzcocks, *Melody Maker* 10/12/77

"Another Movie In A Different Cinema" Feature and interviews, *Sounds* 25/3/78

"Looking Behind The Buzzcocks Myth" Feature *Melody Maker* 25/3/78

"From Front Room To Front Line Of The New Wave" (Feature on drummer John Maher, *Sounds* 3/6/78)

"They Go On And On And On" Two page feature *NME* 17/6/78

"Pete Shelley Is A Sensative Artist....." Two page feature *Melody Maker* 30/9/78

"The Lust Train Stops Here" Two page feature *NME* 14/10/78

"Out of the Kitchen" Buzzcocks in Ireland feature, *Record Mirror* 14/10/78

"Inside The Hit Factory" Two page interview *Sounds* 7/4/79

"True Confessions" Two page feature from Europe, *Record Mirror* 17/3/79

"P.S. I Love You" Two page interview with Pete Shelley, *NME* 28/4/79

"Buzzcocks In New York" Two page feature *Melody Maker* 15/9/79

"Hey Mac, Are You Some Kind O' Limey Pop Star" Feature *NME* 6/10/79

"Sex, Fast Cars And A Different Kind of Buzzcock" Two page interview with Steve Diggle *Sounds* 6/10/79

"Diggle V. Gibson: Guess Who Won" Interview with Diggle, *Melody Maker* 13/10/79

"Has The Pop Plating Worn Off Buzzcocks Silver Spoon?" Two page feature and interview, *NME* 2/11/80

"Ever Fallen Out With Someone?" News feature on split, *NME* 28/3/81

"Somewhere In England" First interview with Shelley after the split, *NME* 4/4/81

BOOKS

It Only Looks As If It Hurts
ISBN 0948 238 089

Black Spring Press (05/94)
The Complete Lyrics 1976-1990
Howard Devoto

BUZZCOCKS FAMILY TREE

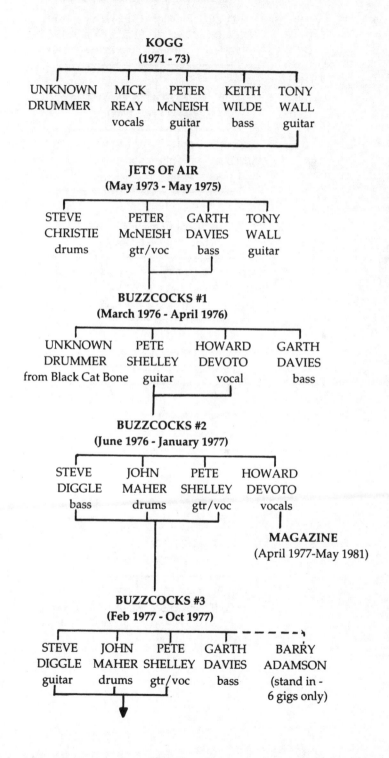

KOGG
(1971 - 73)

UNKNOWN DRUMMER	MICK REAY	PETER McNEISH	KEITH WILDE	TONY WALL
	vocals	guitar	bass	guitar

JETS OF AIR
(May 1973 - May 1975)

STEVE CHRISTIE	PETER McNEISH	GARTH DAVIES	TONY WALL
drums	gtr/voc	bass	guitar

BUZZCOCKS #1
(March 1976 - April 1976)

UNKNOWN DRUMMER	PETE SHELLEY	HOWARD DEVOTO	GARTH DAVIES
from Black Cat Bone	guitar	vocal	bass

BUZZCOCKS #2
(June 1976 - January 1977)

STEVE DIGGLE	JOHN MAHER	PETE SHELLEY	HOWARD DEVOTO
bass	drums	gtr/voc	vocals

MAGAZINE
(April 1977-May 1981)

BUZZCOCKS #3
(Feb 1977 - Oct 1977)

STEVE DIGGLE	JOHN MAHER	PETE SHELLEY	GARTH DAVIES	BARRY ADAMSON
guitar	drums	gtr/voc	bass	(stand in - 6 gigs only)

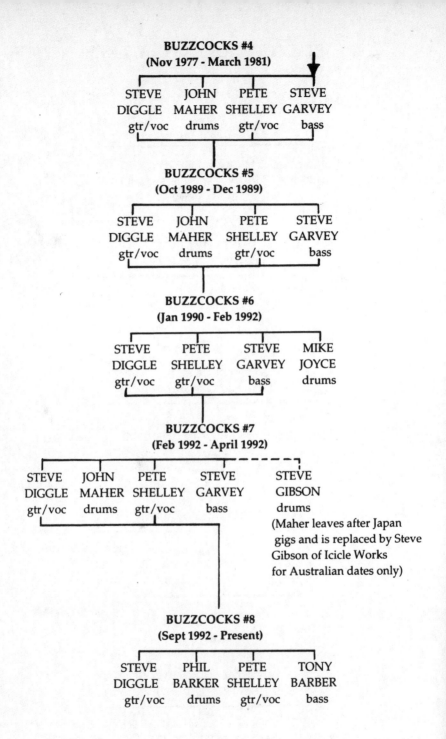

BUZZCOCKS #4
(Nov 1977 - March 1981)

STEVE	JOHN	PETE	STEVE
DIGGLE	MAHER	SHELLEY	GARVEY
gtr/voc	drums	gtr/voc	bass

BUZZCOCKS #5
(Oct 1989 - Dec 1989)

STEVE	JOHN	PETE	STEVE
DIGGLE	MAHER	SHELLEY	GARVEY
gtr/voc	drums	gtr/voc	bass

BUZZCOCKS #6
(Jan 1990 - Feb 1992)

STEVE	PETE	STEVE	MIKE
DIGGLE	SHELLEY	GARVEY	JOYCE
gtr/voc	gtr/voc	bass	drums

BUZZCOCKS #7
(Feb 1992 - April 1992)

STEVE	JOHN	PETE	STEVE	STEVE
DIGGLE	MAHER	SHELLEY	GARVEY	GIBSON
gtr/voc	drums	gtr/voc	bass	drums

(Maher leaves after Japan
gigs and is replaced by Steve
Gibson of Icicle Works
for Australian dates only)

BUZZCOCKS #8
(Sept 1992 - Present)

STEVE	PHIL	PETE	TONY
DIGGLE	BARKER	SHELLEY	BARBER
gtr/voc	drums	gtr/voc	bass